BEYOND THE MIC

Beyond the Mic

Stories from the

Everyday Entrepreneur

ERIC VERDI

BEYOND THE MIC

INTRODUCTION

BEYOND THE MIC
Stories from the Everyday Entrepreneur

© 2018 Eric Verdi Media

All rights reserved. No portion of this book may be reproduced, stored in a retrieval system, or transmitted in any form or by any means—electronic, mechanical, photocopy, recording, scanning, or other—except for brief quotations in critical reviews or articles, without prior written permission of the publisher.

Published by CPS
Printed in the United States of America

ISBN:
ISBN-13:

Limit of liability / Disclaimer of Warranty: While the publisher and author have used their best efforts in preparing this book, they make no representations or warranties regarding the accuracy or completeness of the contents of this book. The publisher and author specifically disclaim any implied warranties or merchantability of fitness for a particular purpose, and make no guarantees whatsoever that you will achieve any particular result. Any case studies that are presented herein do not necessarily represent what you should expect to achieve, since business success depends on a variety of factors. We believe all case studies and results presented herein are true and accurate, but we have not audited the results. The advice and strategies contained in this book may not even be suitable for your situation, and you should consult your own advisors as appropriate. The publisher and author shall not be held liable for any loss of profit or any other commercial damages, including but not limited to special, incidental, consequential, or other damages. The fact that an organization or website is referred to in this work as a citation and/or potential source of information does not mean that the publisher or author endorses the information the organization or website may provide or the recommendations it may make. Further, readers should be aware that Internet websites listed in this work may have changed or disappeared after this work was written.

This publication is designed to provide accurate and authoritative information in regard to the subject matter covered. It is sold with the understanding that the publisher is not engaged in rendering legal, accounting, or other professional services. If legal advice or other expert assistance is required, the services of a competent professional should be sought.

Acknowledgements

After two and a half years of interviewing local business owners and entrepreneurs on my podcast, *Frederick Advice Givers*, I decided that I wanted to share their stories with a broader audience in written format.

These thought leaders and business owners willingly told their stories of triumphs and hardships through that platform. Throughout the 125 episodes and counting, I've found a source of inspiration through each and every one of them.

My source of inspiration for writing this book is Tim Ferriss' *Tools of Titans*. That book is a representation of Tim's own podcast interviews from the billionaires, icons, and world-class performers he has spoken with.

Through this book, I am utilizing a different platform to convey my interviewee's messages to you, the reader.

I want to say how much I appreciate you grabbing a copy of this book and taking the time to read it. I think you will find that by investing your time to learn about the wonderful business owners, thought leaders, and entrepreneurs featured here, you will find inspiration in their stories as well.

I would like to dedicate this book to my wife Susan, our two boys, Anthony and Alex, and my parents.

Without the support of my family and friends the book that you are holding in your hands would never have been able to come to fruition.

It goes without saying that many thanks go out to all those who I've interviewed on *Frederick Advice Givers* and how generous they've been with sharing their struggles, successes, and insights with me.

Most of all, I must thank you, the reader, for picking up *Beyond the Mic*. It's my hope that you gather as much insight and knowledge as I did from listening to these stories.

INTRODUCTION

Preface

BEYOND THE MIC
Stories from the Everyday Entrepreneur

One thing before you read any further and start digging into the content. This book doesn't have to be read from one chapter to the next. Nor do you have to read it section by section.

I found that through interviewing these individuals I was able to learn at least one golden nugget of information from each one. There was a minimum of one takeaway from each one that was thought-provoking, inspirational, or awe-inspiring.

This book was designed to help you pinpoint the topics that are most relevant to you. Read them in any order you wish. Feel free to skip around and have fun! I'm sure that no matter what interviews or chapters you read, you will find that that one nugget of information that provides insight and knowledge regardless of who you are, your background, or profession.

Whether you are looking for tips around the home, investing or finance tips, health and wellness information, or you want to start a business but wondered how others overcame challenges, then this book has something for you.

The information you find inside is meant to be entertaining, educational, and inspirational. I'm certain that anyone can gather insight from my interviewee's stories.

The book is broken up into four sections to help you pick and choose those topics that are of interest to you:

- Home & Finance – Discover tips and information about insurance, investing, finance, fashion, legal services, and real estate.
- Health & Fitness – Learn about getting in shape, medical professionals, alternative health providers, food safety, essential oils, nutrition, and health and beauty products that are good for you and the environment.

- Small Business — Hear the stories of brick and mortar businesses that often started due to a major change in their life and how they started and grew their businesses in spite of obstacles.
- Entrepreneurs — A broader category for those businesses that didn't quite fit into the other areas but who's stories are no less inspiring or amazing that the others.

The chapters are short and concise and taken from a larger context of a 20 to 30-minute full audio interview on *Frederick Advice Givers Podcast*. You may find that one of the chapters strikes a chord and you're interested in learning more about the subject or guest featured. If so, pop on over to iTunes or anywhere Podcasts are played and take a listen. The episode number is in the name of the chapter, so it will be easy for you to find.

Suggested Reading

Beyond the Mic is meant to be a quick and easy read. Each chapter should take you 2-4 minutes and the book does not need to be read from cover to cover. Pick a chapter of your liking and dive in.

Finally, I would love your feedback on our book and welcome your thoughts on my latest project as helping others share their story is a Passion of mine. Email me at BeyondtheMic@EricVerdiMedia.com.

-Eric Verdi

INTRODUCTION

Stories from the Everyday Entrepreneur

I say this on every Podcast. I am the Lucky one. I get to meet these amazing people. Their stories, their tips, their strategies. Each interview I learn something valuable that I can then use in either my business life or personal life.

The reason you are reading *Beyond the Mic* is I wanted you to have the opportunity to meet these amazing people. I am confident that once you read the stories told on the following pages that you will find a few nuggets that you can use.

I want to thank the following guests of Frederick Advice Givers, and thus following contributors in *Beyond the Mic*:

Clare Ahalt	p. 194	Kelsey Freeman	p. 212
Scott Alexander	p. 222	Dr. Josh Funk	p. 156
Stacy Allgood-Smith	p. 200	Chrissy Gemmill	p. 31
Lee Anderson	p. 98	Amy Goldsmith	p. 87
Shari Auldridge	p. 62	Mike Haggerty	p. 56
Rich Austin	p. 197	Whitney Hahn	p. 216
Dr. Alison Bomba	p. 153	Katrin Hallein	p. 59
Darrick Bowens	p. 91	Julie Harris	p. 130
Adam Bradley	p. 237	Dr. Craig Hauser	p. 111
Dani Burkhead	p. 104	Diana Kaye	p. 146
Harold Bussey Jr.	p. 234	Nicole Knight	p. 47
Whitney Carpenter	p. 75	Stacey Krantz	p. 40
Rebecca Carrera	p. 37	Teresa Kuhn	p. 65
Dave Collins	p. 16	Vinny LaBarbera	p. 182
Whitney Dahlberg	p. 25	Katelyn Laflin	p. 118
Kim Dow	p. 188	Jason Lee	p. 206
Danny Farrar	p. 150	Jordan Lewis	p. 228
Mike Fitzgerald	p. 170	Sharon Lopez	p. 22
Caressa Flannery	p. 173	Damion Lupo	p. 72

Monica MacCracken	p. 176	Jamal Rashad	p. 78
Annie Main	p. 166	Joyce Renner	p. 143
Sarah Martucci	p. 127	Janice Riley	p. 240
Jay Mason	p. 191	Rae Roach	p. 140
Chrissy Mayhew	p. 43	Dr. Ashley Russell	p. 124
Cheryle McKee	p. 107	Shabnam Samuel	p. 121
Jessica McHugh	p. 231	Francine Shaw	p. 133
Julie Melton	p. 115	Alex Sincevich	p. 203
Dr. Julio Menocal	p. 94	Ryan Sloper	p. 162
Christina Murphy	p. 136	Aleena Steele	p. 91
Robert Nivens	p. 13	Mark Stevanus	p. 209
Angela Ostroff	p. 179	Monica Stuckey	p. 219
Gabrielle Pastorek	p. 185	Antoine Thomas	p. 225
Erin Pelicano	p. 28	Laura Wallace	p. 200
Earl Pendar	p. 50	Lisa Whidden	p. 6
Chris Popple	p. 9 & 19	Trey Wilkes	p. 243
Sean Quill	p. 69	Dana Young	p. 34

INTRODUCTION

CONTENTS

Section 1 – Introduction	1
Section 2 – Small Business	4
Section 3 – Home & Finance	53
Section 4 – Health & Wellness	85
Section 5 – Entrepreneurship	160
Section 6 – Closing Statement	247

Introduction-

Stories from the Everyday Entrepreneur...

To give you a better understanding of how *Beyond the Mic* came about, I need to start with the story of how *Frederick Advice Givers* originated. It was 2015 and my real estate business had really started to take off on the back of Stories. I was in the midst of researching and writing my first book, *The Psychological Approach to Sell Real Estate,* when I was approached by a local company to advertise in their magazine.

I knew the power of Story and being able to tell your story to create an emotional connection with a larger audience. When I asked the salesperson for the magazine what my 'ad' would look like and if I could 'craft' my own message: the answer was 'NO.'

Knowing through my own personal business that if you can properly tell your story, then you have the power to let people into the inner workings of your world. Thus, Stories from the Every Entrepreneur and the power of Story is something I truly believe.

Frustrated from this experience, I started to think that there was a better way for business owners, entrepreneurs and thought-leaders to get their Story distributed to their audience. When I spoke to my friend and co-founder of *The Frederick Impact Club*, Ryan Fletcher, he told me, "Verdi, what you are going to do is start a Podcast. You are going to interview local business owners and entrepreneurs. And then you will not only be able to distribute the audio Podcast, but you will have articles written for each guest so that they can share their message with their audience in multiple platforms."

Having never listened to a Podcast or even knowing what one was, I had no clue how to start. But Ryan, having a Podcast of his own, helped me start *Frederick Advice Givers.*

INTRODUCTION

For six months I binged on Podcasts such as Entrepreneurs on Fire, Mixergy, and many others to get a feel for how the structure of the interviews would work. I modeled *Frederick Advice Givers* after some of the giants in the Podcasting world and we got off to an incredible start.

The value that our guests had. The feedback they received. The boost in their branding was immediately felt and I knew that I was onto something. Week after week we kept interviewing all these INCREDIBLE people. We got to hear their 'Story' and we got to help them get the word out to a larger audience.

About a year ago, I ordered a copy of the book *Tools of Titans* by Tim Ferris at the recommendation of another friend. The book was a compilation of interviews from Tim's Podcast turned into chapters and thus into a book. I thought, what a GREAT idea, and began on the journey to turn *Frederick Advice Givers* into a book.

Thus, *Beyond the Mic* was born.

I hired a writer, Monique Poché, who normally chooses to remain behind-the-scenes as a ghostwriter, but without her help, it would have taken much longer for this project to come to fruition. I outlined the format for the book and Monique executed the plan perfectly.

Beyond the Mic is meant to be an enjoyable read and to further help *Frederick Advice Givers'* guests share their story in yet a different medium: this book.

BEYOND THE MIC

SECTION ONE

SMALL BUSINESS

I'm a big fan of small business ownership. I think it's the backbone of American innovation. But to be successful, you first have to have the courage to go for it. – Bill Rancic

Small Business

Small Businesses are the heart and soul of America. And nowhere else is this evident than in the Frederick area. Frederick is an amazing town with incredible business owners. What also makes Frederick stand out is that willingness of these small businesses working together to lift each other up in the Entrepreneurial journey.

Without Entrepreneurs having a passion for their business but more importantly their consumers the thriving small business industry would be dead.

This chapter is dedicated to those who have 'shops' and/or run businesses that sell goods to consumers. Some, like Whitney Dahlberg, in downtown Frederick have been in business for over a decade and have carved out an incredible following by offering custom-made, local-made wares. Others like Stacey Krantz of In Bloom Jewelry cater to an entirely different clientele. And although she has a shop/store front, Stacey also has a thriving online business.

Enjoy and frequent these small businesses, because these owners take immense pride in their businesses and without your support their business would not be possible

SMALL BUSINESS

"Dare to live the life you have dreamed for yourself." Ralph Waldo Emerson

---

LISA WHIDDEN

Episode #6 – Lisa Whidden – Owner – Wind & Willow Boutique

Style Tips for Western Wear

Lisa Whidden's (URL: winandwillow.boutique) love of western boots came at an early age when she lived in South Florida. With a rodeo every Friday night, it was difficult to ignore how the boots caught her eye. It was there that she fell in love with the look. Over the years, she's collected lots of vintage boots, and developed quite a collection before opening her shop, Wind & Willow in Downtown Frederick, Maryland. She obtained a degree in Marketing, but prior to opening her store, Lisa worked in retail sales, which is where she originally discovered her love of the fashion industry. Although she did work in banking and management for a while, it was when she had her kids that she realized she wanted to be an entrepreneur. She started with a graphics design business, but she knew she wanted to do something new and exciting in the fashion industry.

Style Tips for Western Wear

Lisa's shop specializes in western boots. She describes her store as one that offers a modern, trendy mix of boots and every day fashion. She strives to carry brands that are moderately priced. The boots she offers are from lines like Lucchese and Corral, which are both handmade, quality products. Since she knows her customers are going to spend a good portion of their money on boots, she still wants them to be able to afford to buy an outfit to go with them. Her focus is on carrying good brands that offer a sophisticated look to fit many different styles and tastes. In addition to selling women's fashion, her store also sells men's boots, sunglasses, jewelry, purses, and a variety of other goods like candles and soaps.

A few style tips from Lisa include:

- It's important to embrace your personal style, whether it be sultry, sexy or sophisticated.
- Don't be afraid to mix it up with textures and colors. It's always good to have a pop of color with what you're wearing.
- Western boots aren't just for winter wear. Many people wear them during other times of the year, especially for summer festivals and concerts.

"Dare to Live the Life You've Always Dreamed Of."

Lisa shared with me that her favorite quote is from Ralph Waldo Emerson. She mentioned that she is all about accepting the dare and going for her dreams. As someone who knows the challenges that come with opening a retail store, I respect her attitude of being able to continue to do just that.

"Never Dwell on Decisions." Ralph Waldo Emerson

Chris Popple

SMALL BUSINESS

Episode #11 – Chris Popple – Owner – Candlelight Floral Designs

Turning a Passion into a Thriving Business

Chris Popple

Chris Popple (URL: CandlelightFloralDesigns.com) started his business based on a challenge that came up while planning his wedding. Melissa, his then fiancé, wanted to have something unique for the table centerpieces at the reception. She decided on tropical fish tanks based on their time spent diving in Australia. When both the hotel and the wedding planner decided against helping out with this unique request, it was up to Chris and his groomsmen to put everything together the morning of the ceremony. The compliments were so overwhelming that they started doing it for others as a business. At first, Melissa was running the business by herself while Chris was working in the pharmaceutical industry. But after a few moves and settling in the United States, he decided to join Melissa in their business, Candlelight Floral Designs.

Turning a Passion into a Thriving Business

As the owner of a company in the floral industry, it can be a challenge to maintain a healthy variety of flowers throughout the year. However, that doesn't stop Chris in the off-season months. While local flowers are abundant during the summer months, it's the winter months where he has to look elsewhere to have an adequate supply on hand. He looks to the southern states like Florida, Georgia, and Louisiana or for the more tropical flowers, he can obtain supply from Central and South America. It's this level of dedication that reflects Chris' dedication to his business and his customers.

What impresses me most with Chris is not just his passion for his business, but his passion for helping his customers in any situation. He shared a story with me about a local bride who was having trouble finding a florist who wanted just a bouquet for her wedding. Most of the local florists were requiring her to do a minimum order of a few thousand dollars. She ended up contacting Chris, and he was happy to oblige and provide her with a beautiful bouquet. But the story doesn't end there. The bride was so happy with the service she received that she ended up referring about two dozen other clients to him!

Candlelight Floral Designs also holds bridal DIY classes for those who want to add their own personal touch to their wedding. In these circumstances, they turn the shop over to the wedding party, give them access to a florist, provide space in their cooler, along with workspace to design and create their arrangements. There are even times where the wedding photographer will join them to take pictures of the event! It's just one of the ways Chris and Melissa cater to their clientele and make sure they have the best experience possible.

Inspired by Entrepreneur Sir Richard Branson

Being from the UK, it's only natural for Chris to pick fellow countryman Richard Branson as one of his biggest inspirations. Chris has found both Branson's books, *Losing My Virginity* and *Screw It, Let's Do It*, as resources that he turns to for his business. He likes that Branson believes that you should never dwell on a decision. You should never regret doing something; only regret not doing it. Chris also reads his blog and Twitter posts because the content makes you think about how you're doing things and how you can improve. It's also important as business owners and entrepreneurs to understand that you may not get it right the first time. You don't have to be perfect, just do it and refine the process along the way.

SMALL BUSINESS

Fun Facts About Chris

- Chris and Melissa met in college even though their studies were very different, and they had an unlikely possibility of meeting. Her major was Music, and his was Biology.
- They have lived in the UK, Australia, Southeast Asia, the Caribbean, and areas around the United States.
- Was told by *Washingtonian Bride & Groom Magazine* that their business is a cross between *Downton Abbey* and *The Great Gatsby*.

"What do I fear? I fear stagnation and lack of progress. I fear never reaching my potential and being average. I fear being forgotten...the past...yesterday's news. I fear giving up and being passed by, going softly into that good night. I fear settling, giving into the "that's just the way it is" mindset. I fear dying without leaving my mark. And most of all, I fear NOT feeling these fears anymore..." Unknown

---

ROBERT NIVENS

SMALL BUSINESS

Episode #19 – Robert Nivens – Owner – Bioactive Neutralizer

Overcoming Challenges to Provide for Your Community

Robert Nivens

Robert Nivens (URL: http://bioactivefresh.com/ Email: robert@bioactivefresh.com) has a unique background that instantly reflects his ability to overcome life's unexpected challenges. At 14, his parents gave him up, and he was forced into foster care. Given such a difficult adjustment, Robert ended up running away and living on the streets. At 17, he entered the military for three years. When he was done with his service, Robert had a career in sales, then moved into the finance industry for 30 years. During this time, he helped people with insurance, investing in stocks and bonds, and mortgages. When the financial crisis hit in 2008, he lost his job and spent a few years figuring out what his next move would be. It was when a friend introduced him to biotechnology that his life made a positive and dramatic change.

How Every Day Challenges Created a Need for Business and Philanthropy

When people hear about Robert's business, Bioactive Neutralizer, they realize one of two things. Either they're instantly amazed at the technology involved, or they're worried about just how clean their home, car, or workplace really is! Bioactive Neutralizer uses technology to eliminate biological footprints. This means things that none of us want to come in contact with: bacteria, viruses, pathogens, germs, mold, mildew, allergens, and chemicals. All of these are becoming more resistant to disinfectants and antibiotics, which causes a serious problem for the population. So think of your home, when you buy a used car, go to a hospital or doctor's office, or send your kids to daycare, and you can understand how we can come into contact with any of these at any given time.

Robert's business has developed a technology that eliminates the threat that these organisms create. And what makes this even more amazing, is that they can do this in a way that is 100% biodegradable. It can be safely used around humans, pets, plants, and there are no adverse side effects. Doing this type of work is very important to Robert. It's great for him to see how it's helped people overcome both physical and neurological health problems, and it helps the environment at the same time.

What I think is interesting in Robert's case is that his generosity expands beyond his company and into the community. He likes to do mentoring and helping the youth through his work with Manassas House. As someone who was once in foster care, he knows that a child is removed from the system at the age of 18. This can be a traumatic experience as they often have nowhere to go or the money to provide for themselves. They are also at risk for homelessness, drug and alcohol abuse, suicide, and incarceration. At the Manassas House, they welcome young men between the ages of 18 and 26 who have been in foster care. They can live there for six months to up to 2 years. While they reside in the house, they also receive training, mentoring, and personal finance guidance.

They are looking to open up an additional Manassas House so that young men can have a place where they go to get the support they need to survive in the world.

SMALL BUSINESS

"Be Patient. Give it Your All and It Will Be Fine."

DAVE COLLINS

Episode #22 – Dave Collins – Master Winemaker – Big Cork Vineyards

Inside the World of Winemaking

Dave Collins

With over 30 years of experience in horticulture, it's no surprise that Dave Collins (URL: http://www.bigcorkvineyards.com/) earns a living by making wine. He studied horticulture at Virginia Tech and spent his early career working in the greenhouse industry growing nursery plants. For the last 30 years, he's focused on growing grapes and making wine. He originally started out in Virginia but has now transitioned into Maryland at Big Cork Vineyards. His vineyard has won numerous awards since opening in January of 2015. Among them are Best in Show at the 2015 Maryland Governor's Cup Competition for their 2013 Petit Verdot, and their 2014 Chardonnay has won five awards across the country, including the MD Winemasters Best in Show.

Inside the World of Winemaking

As you might expect, many components go into growing grapes and eventually turning them into wine. Dave explained to me that winemaking isn't a quick process. Planting takes place in the spring. If the plants are nurtured and cared for properly, the first crop will happen in the third year from planting. During that time and for the life of the plant, factors such as rainfall, soil, and temperatures can all impact the grapes and eventually the winemaking process.

Dave says that what most people don't realize is that different grapes require different processing. For instance, the grapes for white wine don't go through the same steps as those do for red wine. The process will also vary depending on the type of wine, whether it be a chardonnay or merlot.

For a white wine, the grapes are harvested, chilled down, crushed and pressed. The juice is then pumped into a tank, where it is fermented slowly with yeast. If a semi-dry wine is being made, the fermenting is stopped before all the sugars turn into alcohol. This process allows for some of the natural sugars to remain in the wine.

For a red wine, the process becomes more involved. Before harvesting takes place, it's essential that the grapes are fully matured. This means that red grapes stay on the vine much longer than grapes used for white wine. Once the red grapes are harvested, they are chilled and crushed, but not pressed. The crushed grapes are de-stemmed, and the remainder of the grape product or must, is pumped to a tank to ferment with the skin intact. After fermentation is complete, it is then pressed and transferred to barrels where it will age 18 to 20 months before bottling.

Creating a Customer Experience with Wine

Dave proclaims himself to be a '70s guy, and a book that resonates with him is *Zen and the Art of Motorcycle Maintenance* by Robert M. Pirsig. It may sound like a unique source of inspiration, but Dave makes a great comparison to how the book actually reflects the entire process of making wine.

The book is about how the narrator traveled with his son on a cross-country motorcycle trip. Along the way, they're faced with being outdoors, facing the elements, and fixing up the bike along the way. Dave says that this reflects winemaking in that you are dealing with weather, being outdoors, and making changes along the way. All of these components come together to create an experience for the customer that goes beyond just the wine. The vineyard offers fresh air, beautiful mountain views where the customer can enjoy a glass of wine, great food, and have the perfect escape from the modern world.

"Look at what you can do better."

CHRIS POPPLE

Episode #23 – Chris Popple – Co-Owner – Candlelight Floral Designs

How Resources and Referrals Grow Your Business

Chris Popple

You may recognize Chris Popple's (URL: https://candlelightfloraldesigns.com/) name from an earlier chapter. In fact, I've included Chris here a second time directly because of our previous encounter. After the original podcast episode aired of our original conversation, something wonderful happened. Other businesses and individuals who heard that podcast started contacting Chris to inquire about his services. Chris had contacted me to thank me for the experience, but I also wanted to share that something else can be learned from this.

Using Different Resources to Attract Referrals and Grow Your Business

While you can learn more about Chris and his business in Chapter 11, I want to use what happened after the podcast as a way to help other businesses grow. Of course, being on any podcast will help you gain exposure. The difference here is that when Chris participated in that episode, he did something that he hadn't thought of doing before and as a result, he attracted many referrals within his community.

So many of us who are business owners get bogged down by all that we need to do. We have to run the business, take care of our customers, manage any staff, and market our products and services. What happens is that we get stuck doing the same thing over and over without knowing if it's the right thing to do or if it's working.

In Chris's case, he had never done a podcast before. But that one 15-minute interview made a significant impact on his business. His potential customers had the opportunity to learn more about Chris, how he started his business, and how he takes special care with his customers all in his own voice. If you think about it, most people buy based on who they know and trust, so it's really not that surprising that his business expanded due to that podcast interview.

Regardless of the methods you use to promote your business, you should be consistently finding ways to let your customers know about you to build trust and credibility. Even in our follow up conversation, Chris mentioned how he goes above and beyond to provide a great customer experience. For example, he'll work with a realtor to coordinate when a couple gets the keys to their new home and have flowers delivered at exactly the same moment. Often, they will recognize him as he's the one who did the flowers for their wedding!

Chris also took step to have his website redesigned as his customers wanted a way to order directly online. Now, 90% of his orders come from his site. Not only does this provide convenience to his customers, but it also frees up time that his staff was spending on the phone taking orders.

It's great to provide a personal touch for your customers. However, to benefit from it, they have to know about it. Referrals will definitely help spread the word but putting yourself out there in different formats can speed the process along.

SMALL BUSINESS

"Money will come if you're passionate about what you do."

SHARON LOPEZ

Episode #24 – Sharon Lopez – Franchise Owner – Money Mailer

Five Tips for Growing Your Business

Sharon Lopez

Sharon Lopez (Email: sharonlopez@moneymailer.com) spent many years in corporate management consulting. She traveled and worked long hours to help Fortune 100 companies make a profit through Customer Relationship Management systems. After having kids, she realized she couldn't maintain that pace and wanted to be there more for them. She quit and became a yoga instructor while her husband started investing in real estate. This transition changed her life and helped her to figure out what's really important.

Even though she was tempted to stay in a corporate job along with the lure of a large salary and expense accounts, she knew that her kids were growing up fast and she didn't want to miss out on key events in their life. That's when she decided to buy a Money Mailer franchise. With it, she can take her 20 years of experience with helping big businesses turn a profit and use it to help small businesses become successful while helping her community at the same time.

5 Tips for Growing Your Business

Sharon shared with me that her experience as a yoga instructor made her realize their biggest challenge when it comes to success. All too often, a person's mind and thoughts are the biggest obstacles. It's by taking the time to quiet the mind through activities like yoga or meditation that you can envision your success.

Here are Sharon's five tips for growing your business:

- Have a good customer acquisition strategy - it's easy to get busy and think we have enough going on with our existing customer base. However, people move all the time, so it's

important to actively attract new customers and introduce them to your business. You have to constantly be in front of them and the best avenues are with direct mail, TV, and radio advertising.
- Build brand recognition – figure out what makes your business unique? Do you have a special warranty or guarantee? Do you have a unique process or formula?
- Know the value of a customer – most small businesses don't take the time to understand the value of a customer. It's important to figure out your ideal customer, how often they visit your place of business, and what they are spending on a weekly, monthly, or yearly basis.
- Have a catch to get the customer in the door. Give them something to compel them to act. This can be something like free shipping or a buy one, get one free offer.
- Make sure your product is in front of your audience. Who is your ideal customer? What do they buy? Are they buying for themselves or their family? Do they have a home? A car?

Books That Have Shaped Her Career Transition

Angela credits two books that helped her transition from a career in corporate to owning her business. The first is *Rich Dad, Poor Dad* by Robert Kiyosaki. It was written at the beginning of the real estate investment trend, and it gave her the seeds to what would it take to own a business and succeed. It also gave her the keys to financial success for her and her family without having to rely on a traditional job.

The other book that Sharon mentions is what she used as the basis for her yoga foundation, *The Yoga Sutras of Patanjali* by Swami Satchidananda. She considers it a foundational text for most self-help resources that are available on the market and that it was life-changing for her.

"There is a Difference between Buying Local vs Big Business"

WHITNEY DAHLBERG

SMALL BUSINESS

Episode #25 – Whitney Dahlberg – Owner – The Muse

Whitney Dahlberg

Always interested in art and fashion, Whitney Dahlberg (URL: http://shopthemuse.com/) was destined to have her own retail shop. At a young age, she enjoyed taking classes, especially in sewing, and that's when she developed a love for fashion design. Her parents allowed her to go to New York when she was 16 where she attended Parsons and spent the summer doing college courses in fashion design. Although she loved it, she also realized that it was a bit too cutthroat for her, so she was unsure of what her next steps would be. After graduating from college at the University of Pittsburgh, she went into retail, merchandise management, and retail management.

While working in her career, Whitney sewed on the side and did a lot of soul-searching before she came to the conclusion that she wanted to open her own business. She was hesitant at first given the risk, but she took the leap anyway. When Whitney opened her store, she sold items she liked and wanted to shop for as well as goods that she had made. She took business management classes, created a 40-page business plan, and applied for a loan with local banks. She also made sure to wait until just the right time to acquire the perfect location in Downtown Frederick.

Why You Should Buy Local vs. Big Business

Whitney is a role model for other business owners who want to give back to their community. She and a friend started a charity called Lend a Hand that raises money for student homelessness. She also features work from other local artists in her store. These are just a few of the many reasons why she states that consumers should buy local instead of going to the bigger chain stores.

When you shop at a local store, you can support your community on multiple levels. The items are handmade by one of your neighbors, so you're helping to support their craft too. In fact, Whitney says that about 70% of the items in her store are locally made.

Also, by shopping locally, you have much more insight into the products you buy. Not only do you know that it's made in the U.S., but you can also learn the story of the person behind the product. You can ask about why they made the item, how it was made, and what was used to make it.

Buying from a local store also gives you a unique look. When you shop at a big box or department store, you run the risk of running into someone who has the exact same shirt or outfit as you do. At a local store, the items are more one-of-a-kind. You'll likely find something that won't be found anywhere else. People will also be more likely to compliment you on your purchase due to its unique style.

A Workbook for Creatives

As you've read, Whitney put a lot of effort into preparing to open her business. She also used a book called *Creating a Life Worth Living* by Carol Lloyd as part of her preparation. It acts as a workbook for creatives and helps them find their success. The book shows how people are taught in school how to be a doctor or accountant, but if you're a creative, you're left with not being sure of what to do.

For Whitney, the book was a great resource for her as it made her realize that she wanted to open a store. It made her think a lot about herself and her future. It's also a resource that she recommends to any students interested in a creative venture who come into her store.

SMALL BUSINESS

"I will believe it when I see it."

ERIN PELICANO

Episode #27 – Erin Pelicano – Jewelry Designer

How a Layoff Created a Successful Jewelry Brand

Erin Pelicano

Even though Erin Pelicano (URL: https://www.erinpelicano.com/) had a career in civil engineering, she never lost her love for doing creative things. It was her love of math and solving problems that led to engineering, but she was also torn between fashion design and architecture in school. When changes started happening to the economy, it also started to negatively affect her career, and she wanted to focus on her children. It wasn't long before she was laid off, which forced her and her husband to think outside of the box.

How a Layoff Created a Successful Jewelry Brand

Erin and her husband took a jewelry class, so they already had the tools and knowledge to start the business. Combining that knowledge with her creative side allowed Erin to hit the ground running. She started out by making Christmas gifts for her friends and family. She also brought some pieces to The Muse (see Chapter #25), and she started an online Etsy store. Although the business was slow to grow in the beginning, it picked up speed with the help of posts on Pinterest. Once the business became more successful, Erin's husband quit his job, and now they work together.

Given that she has an online business, it was difficult for her in the beginning to separate time for her family and time for work. She's now worked it out so that she can step away from the business and focus on family when needed. She also feels that it's good for her kids to see her running a business and how that can positively influence them as they grow older. Although, Erin does say that it's

SMALL BUSINESS

difficult to keep up with all the ever-changing technology when you run an online business.

Erin feels that her being laid off is the best thing that could ever happen to her. You can plan all you want and expect for your life to go in a specific direction, but you never know what surprises are in store for us.

Through the jewelry that Erin and her husband create, they can build a personal connection with their customers. The customers know where the jewelry is made, who made it, the meaning behind it, and can be assured that the product is made in the U.S. They also can make jewelry that is customer-centric and tailored to fit a specific event or occurrence in their life.

"I Will See It When I Believe It"

This quote is one that resonates with Erin. She says that it's important to believe in whatever you're dreaming of, whether it's your personal life, business, or relationships. Try to have a positive outlook and believe that something is going to happen.

BEYOND THE MIC

"Life if Fragile; Love is Not."

CHRISSY GEMMILL

SMALL BUSINESS

Episode #29 – Chrissy Gemmill – Jewelry Designer

Using a Platform to Raise Autism Awareness

Chrissy Gemmill

It was living in a peaceful, serene setting as a child that Chrissy Gemmill (URL: https://www.etsy.com/people/ChrissyGemmillJewels) attributes to her creative side. She says it was this environment that didn't include the internet or neighbors close-by that caused her to play and make up things to do outside. She also had a passion for jewelry, which caused her mom to sign her up for a class when she was 15. This led her to start her jewelry business in high school as she loved to create things for people to wear.

Chrissy found fulfillment in jewelry making and became obsessed with it. In college, she also studied metalsmithing. With these skills and the fact that she wanted to work for herself, she built her own jewelry business. Now, she's surrounded with things she loves. She can work her own hours, and be there for her family.

Using a Platform to Raise Autism Awareness

Chrissy admits that it's a challenge to take time for the administrative tasks that come with owning a business. She's now hired a bookkeeper so that she can manage her time for more important things.

Mainly, it frees up more of her time, so she can be available for her son who has autism. With her business, she has the flexibility to care for him when needed. In addition to being able to choose her own hours, she also has a platform that she can use to raise awareness for autism to help others in her community.

In fact, she has teamed up with other artists in the area, and they often do fundraisers. These events will often provide much-needed devices or other items to benefit the autism community. One time it provided tracking devices that were distributed to those who have communication issues.

Chrissy will also create jewelry pieces to help her customers get through a stressful time. For example, she made a bracelet for a customer whose son was being re-evaluated. Her customer told her that the bracelet offered a source of inspiration as she was going through such a difficult time.

Regardless of the reason behind the pieces she creates, Chrissy knows that people wear jewelry because it makes them feel good. They can use a piece to adorn themselves in something beautiful and brighten their day.

Like most handmade goods, her pieces are made with love. A lot of thought and meaning is behind her work, and she will often incorporate a gemstone or crystal to enhance the power of an individual piece.

Staying Organized & Living to the Fullest

For those of us who run a business, it can be a challenge to get work done while staying on top of everything else that needs to get done. The book *Eat That Frog* by Brian Tracy is what Chrissy used as a workbook to help prioritize her day and stay organized.

When Chrissy made a bracelet for a customer, who wanted the phrase, "Life is fragile, love is not" inscribed on the piece. The phrase resonated with her and taught her to live each day with love, live each day to the fullest and don't take anything for granted.

"Success consists of going from failure to failure without loss of enthusiasm." Winston Churchill

DANA YOUNG

Episode #34 – Dana Young – Jewelry Design

Contributing to Causes with Your Brand

Dana Young

As a kid, Dana Young (https://danayoungjewelry.com/) felt out of place as a city girl in the suburbs of Boston. She was a self-proclaimed "punky nerd" who loved the arts, always dressed different, had colored hair, and was obsessed with nature. It wasn't a surprise to anyone when she left home to go to art school in Brooklyn. She ended up working in corporate fashion jewelry but found it to be a very stressful environment.

Contributing to Causes with Your Brand

As with quite a few of the entrepreneurs I've met, Dana fell into entrepreneurship by accident. She was working at a job that she thought would be a great opportunity, but it wasn't what she expected. She has been working there for ten months when a co-worker asked her if she would every start her own business. Two hours later, both of them were laid off, which she absolutely took as a sign!

One of the many great things about Dana's business is that a percentage of her profits goes to animal and environmental welfare organizations. It perfectly reflects how entrepreneurs can make a difference in the world and their community as they have the power to follow their passions.

Dana also loves the fact that her business connects her with like-minded people. One of her regular customers works for an animal rescue, where she removes dogs and cats from bad situations. She then puts those animals in a good home. On a rescue trip, the client was wearing a necklace from Dana's collection, and one of the client's coworkers admired it. She said that it looked like a key to a magical land where no animal cruelty exists. It's stories like this that make her realize that she is reaching the right people and benefitting causes that are important to her.

Inspiration from Winston Churchill & Harry Potter

It may seem strange to gather inspiration from two such differing sources, but in Dana's world, they make perfect sense.

The Winston Churchill quote, "Success consists of going from failure to failure without loss of enthusiasm," is one that Dana feels should be something for every entrepreneur to be reminded of and draw inspiration from.

Dana also mentioned that the *Harry Potter series* by J.K. Rowling is something that she personally connects with. She feels that the books and others like them should serve to remind people that it's okay to dream and be childish sometimes. It's okay to be transported by any form of art, which is similar to how she feels about the purpose of her jewelry line.

"Never, Ever, Ever Give Up!"

REBECCA CARRERA

SMALL BUSINESS

Episode #38 – Rebecca Carrera – Maven Beauty Bar

Why Healthy Beauty Products are Important for You and the Environment

Rebecca Carrera

Rebecca Carrera (URL: https://www.mavenbeautybar.com/) started her business because she wanted women to have a place where they could shop for makeup, skin care, and cosmetics without it being an intimidating experience. Unlike most department stores where salespeople can be too pushy, Maven Beauty Bar offers an atmosphere that makes shoppers feel like they are hanging out with friends or at someone's home. They also have a policy to not sell items that a customer doesn't need.

Like a lot of entrepreneurs, Rebecca was worried about leaving behind the "safety" of a corporate job. She decided to start her store as a pop-up inside of another store to see what would happen. As business picked up, she decided to open up her own store with its own boutique-feel.

Why Healthy Beauty Products are Important for You and the Environment

Maven Beauty Bar specializes in natural beauty products and services including eyebrow threading, makeup lessons, and makeup applications. The products they use are natural, local brands that are toxin-free or free of the top-known toxins. Their team tries out the products before they are put on the shelves, and they don't sell anything they wouldn't use, or 100% believe in.

It was important for Rebecca to have this mindset for her store as she knows that most products available aren't necessarily safe. For her, it's not just about how a product looks or feels. It's more about how that product reacts to your body internally. Certain mainstream products have dangerous chemicals in them and aren't safe for your body. Her focus is on helping people to stay away from those types of products.

They also sell other non-beauty products like glass water bottles that are not only safer for you, but they also help to protect the environment. In addition to beauty products, they talk about topics like healthy living, yoga, and exercise to give customers a more comprehensive way to naturally improve their health. Overall, they want their customers to have a healthy beauty experience.

Rebecca loves that she gets to make such an impact on her customer's lives. They can feel better about themselves through using the products she sells while also protecting their health. It's also great to be able to start young girls in a positive environment that will carry them throughout their lives.

"Never, Ever, Ever Give Up."

Rebecca is grateful that her dad always believed in whatever she set out to do. It's his words of never giving up that stay with her even when faced with challenges. That quote along with, "This too shall pass" show her that even if there's a bump in the road or it feels like there's no way out, it's going to be okay. Things can change in the blink of an eye. Our situation can change at any moment and turn things around.

"We are what we repeatedly do. Excellence, then, is not an act, it is a habit." – Aristotle

STACEY KRANTZ

Episode #44 – Stacey Krantz – In Bloom Jewelry

How Our Paths Can Naturally Lead Us to Our Calling

Stacey Krantz

Stacey Krantz (https://inbloomjewelry.com/) is a fourth generation Fredericktownian on both her mother and father's side. Both of them were very respected and revered educators in the community. In fact, not only do I remember her parents, but during my conversation with her, I realized that we have quite a few friends in common.

How Our Paths Can Naturally Lead Us to Our Calling

Stacey started out on a very different path from the one she's currently on. She graduated from college with a degree in Social Work and applied for the Peace Corp. She was sent to Gabon, Africa where she taught farmers how to raise tilapia fish. But it was the women who inspired her. She recognized how industrious they were and how they made the most of what they had.

Her social work then took her to an Indian reservation in New Mexico where she worked as a counselor for kids. It was during her work there that she met a goldsmith and became interested in making her own jewelry. Given that both her parents were creative, it wasn't a stretch for her to love her new hobby.

Even though she had found this new interest, she continued on her path to getting a Masters in Social Work, but then things took an interesting turn. She knew she would need to take a side job to help get herself through school. Instead of taking a traditional part-time job, she decided to sell the pieces she was making at Eastern Market in D.C. It brought in enough money, so she just kept going for the next 2 – 3 years.

With her success at selling her jewelry, she was invited to attend a wholesale event where she could have access to a bigger audience. In spite of her hesitation, she was able to make more at that one show than she would have made in one year as a social worker. Needless to say, she quit school and turned all of her focus towards making and selling jewelry.

I hear so many stories just like Stacey's when I talk to entrepreneurs. Most were on a certain path, and just one change of events made a major difference in their lives. It's by paying attention to these types of opportunities and events and expanding our horizons that can help us to make a change or switch directions for the better. It will often lead to something that we're passionate about that we hadn't considered before, which can make all the difference in enjoying our work and what we do for a living.

If you look at Stacey's story, she's still able to help people. It just happens to be in a different and more creative way. Creating jewelry for a specific event or person can be extremely rewarding. It can be a way to memorialize someone or something that can be passed down for generations. Stacey is also able to use her business as a platform to recognize important people in the community, which I think is a vital part of being an entrepreneur.

"People are often unreasonable, irrational, and self-centered. Forgive them anyway. If you are kind, people may accuse you of selfish, ulterior motives. Be kind anyway. If you are successful, you will win some unfaithful friends and some genuine enemies. Succeed anyway. If you are honest and sincere people may deceive you. Be honest and sincere anyway. What you spend years creating, others could destroy overnight. Create anyway. If you find serenity and happiness, some may be jealous. Be happy anyway. The good you do today will often be forgotten. Do good anyway. Give the best you have, and it will never be enough. Give your best anyway. In the final analysis between you and God, it's never between you and them anyway." Mother Teresa

---

CHRISSY MAYHEW

SMALL BUSINESS

Episode #57 – Chrissy Mayhew – Heartland Payment Systems

The Importance of Paying Attention to Your Customer's Needs

Chrissy Mayhew

As a child, Chrissy Mayhew (https://www.heartlandpaymentsystems.com/) was a tomboy, loved sports, and being outside. Part of this love developed from spending time on her grandparent's farm in Minnesota where she lived in the summers to help out. At the University of Maryland, she studied interior design, construction management, and business management. Later when her husband started a construction business, her experience led to her being able to help with drafting, managing the sites, and doing administrative tasks like bookkeeping.

When the economy crashed around 2010, their business slowed, and Chrissy realized that she would need to go back to work. She was connected to the local BNI for the construction business, and it was through the people she met there that she was able to find a new opportunity. She was already using Heartland Payment Systems, a credit card processing company, for the construction business. It was a representative for them that she knew from the BNI meetings that recommended she try selling for a change. At first, she was hesitant, but she saw the benefits of joining the company, especially because it allowed her to have a flexible schedule.

The Importance of Paying Attention to Your Customer's Needs

Chrissy didn't want to be perceived along the lined of a "sleazy car salesman" when she went into sales. But she realized that her job was much more than selling to people; it was about paying attention to their needs and providing them with a solution.

When Chrissy meets with a potential client, she views it as an educational session. She sits down with them to determine what options are best for their situation. As her clients are also members of her community, she sees her work as a way to build relationships with them. Chrissy believes that the 3 key ingredients to any successful relationship is "Know, Like and Trust". Most people feel more at ease when you get to know them better. Maybe find some things you have in common. The more you know about each other, the more they "like and trust" you to do business with them. Once the trust is built, they also want to refer you to their family and friends.

Most of the time, Heartland can give her customers lower fees and save them money. But again, it's also about relationships. So many of her customers appreciate the fact that she's local and accessible to them. Many other credit card processing companies don't have a local representative and often only have customer service teams overseas.

Chrissy also gives her potential clients a questionnaire that takes them through important factors they need to know about taking credit cards as a form of payment for their business. In some cases, it will show that it's not a good idea for them. By learning about her customers through this strategy, she can determine their frustrations, needs, and wants to come up with a solution for them. And even though that sometimes means her services aren't right for them, she is still able to provide them with business tips or other solutions that can serve them.

Tips for Business and Selling

Chrissy points to the book, *Rich Dad, Poor Dad* by Robert Kiyosaki as the book that helped her and her husband run their construction business. After that book, they read the rest of the series, and it turned their minds towards key things about running a business that they hadn't thought of. The tips in those books also helped Chrissy with embracing sales when she started with Heartland. One thing that stands out with her is that the books are helpful to anyone who doesn't know about a lot about business.

"The best Exercise for a Person is to Reach Down and Pick Someone Else Up."

NICOLE KNIGHT

SMALL BUSINESS

Episode #65 – Nicole Knight – Smooch

Empowering Women One Lipstick at a Time

Nicole Knight

Nicole Knight (http://www.smoochstudio.com/) had the fortune to have parents that encouraged her pursuits. She was taught from a young age to be the very best at whatever she wanted to do, and the sky would be the limit. They also taught her that by living her life with integrity and purpose, she could achieve any goal.

Nicole was a teacher for a couple of years in the early '90s. It was during that time that she met a dynamic businesswoman, Faye, who had her own makeup company. She initially got experience in the salon industry as her brother-in-law worked in the business. He asked her to bring makeup into the salon since she was shadowing Faye and learning everything she needed to know about the business side of makeup. It became a natural thing for her, and she pulled her line into the salon.

Although Nicole continued to teach for four more years, she knew the makeup business was what she wanted to do. She eventually took a full-time job with Faye and then ventured out with her own line. She expanded her line to more salons and started growing her business, Smooch! Studio.

Empowering Women One Lipstick at a Time

Through her work, Nicole realized she had discovered a need where women weren't confident with what they were doing with their makeup. Either they had learned from their mom or sister or they had just figured it out on their own. That's when she knew she could combine her teaching talents with her makeup business.

Her goal, along with her sister-in-law who co-owns the business, is to educate clients on why they're doing what they're doing. It was in the winter of 2008 that they were seeking out what their next steps should be, and they decided on opening up their own store.

Even though they opened their store in April 2009, at the height of the economy crash, their business flourished due to the "lipstick effect." When the economy is bad, smaller items like lipstick will sell well because it's a luxurious necessity, it's affordable, and it's a pick-me-up item. Women will wear makeup no matter what the economy does.

What helps them to stand out from other cosmetics is that they can create customized makeup for each of their clients. They offer a solution for all demographics in an affordable way with clean, botanical-based products. As Nicole points out, everybody has skin, and it's important to take care of it. It's their job to look at their client's skin and create products to match shades, types, and personalities.

They are also very strict about the integrity of the ingredients they use in their products. Whatever you put on your skin is absorbed within 45 seconds, and it goes directly into your bloodstream. With so many harmful chemicals in most cosmetics, they strive to provide clean, healthy options for their clients.

For Nicole, the most important part of their business is their mission to empower women to see themselves as beautiful on the inside and the outside. They work with women from 9 to 99 years old and offer age-appropriate solutions according to style and lifestyle. Their solutions are created to match a routine that makes sense to their individual client.

Doing Something Small Every Day

A book that Nicole refers to as one that's important to her is *The Slight Edge* by Jeff Olson. It explains how just doing something once won't affect us one way or another. But, if we do something for ourselves or our business every day, even if it's small, it will create big results over time.

SMALL BUSINESS

"The Hippie of Hair."

EARL PINDAR

BEYOND THE MIC

Episode #72 – Earl Pindar – Natural Fusion Hair Studio

Embracing the Concept of an Eco-Friendly Hair Salon

Earl Pindar

As so often happens in sports, a football injury led Earl Pindar (http://www.naturalfusionhairstudio.com/) to seek out a different avenue for his career as he wasn't able to play anymore. Although you wouldn't think going into hairdressing would be a natural transition, he loves that it's a way for him to be artistic and meet a variety of people. His title "Hippie of Hair" comes from his love of the outdoors, nature, animals, as well as his focus on having an eco-friendly business.

Embracing the Concept of an Eco-Friendly Hair Salon

Earl met his wife, Kelly, in California where he's from. However, she's from the Frederick area and wanted to be closer to her family. They took a 3-month road trip to drive from the West Coast to the East Coast and along the way they hashed out an idea and business plan for a salon, Natural Fusion Hair Studio.

Once they arrived in Frederick, they got a house in downtown, and renovated the lower level into a salon and made the upstairs portion their living area. It took a year of hard work to put it all together, but it paid off as they've just celebrated ten years in business.

While some people may just think of this business as just another beauty parlor, it's not your typical salon. First, Earl's entire team is geared towards educating their clients. When they meet with a client for the first time, they go through an extensive consultation. During this meeting, they discover what the client is looking for, any challenges they have with their hair, as well as what attracted them to the salon.

The main thing that they've discovered is that people come to the salon due to is its core focus on being an eco-friendly business. However, this is a concept that's just as important to their clients as it is to their staff. As Earl points out, hairdressers are second in line to coal miners for contracting lung disease. The chemicals can be so high in a typical hair salon that they can cause health problems as well as allergic reactions that can be career ending.

At Earl's salon, they want to leave the smallest carbon footprint possible as a result of the work they do. They have removed a lot of the products that contain harsh chemicals found in hair care products such as hair dyes with ammonia. Instead, they have replaced those and other products with professional hair care lines that are certified organic and offer more gentle, sustainable options. His team also works together to go out of their way to reuse or recycle materials instead of just washing products down the drain. He attributes these practices to what will help him run his business for many more years to come without the health concerns that other hair stylists face.

Driving Business with Leadership

The book, *No-Compromise Leadership* by Neil Ducoff, is one that has made an impact on Earl and his business. It's helped him to develop a great view of his business. Even as a hair salon, he still has the same struggles and challenges as other business, and this book has helped him to keep driving and growing his salon.

BEYOND THE MIC

HOME & FINANCE

Price is what you Pay. Value is what you Get. – Warren Buffett

Introduction- Home and Finance

There are many books that I have read to help direct me towards a better financial mindset. If you are looking for a better way to manage your finances, then I recommend reading the three books listed at the end of this page that have changed my outlook on finances.

The interviewees in this chapter range from mortgage lenders to title companies to insurance agents to wealth management experts who manage portfolios in the hundreds of millions of dollars.

Each guest in this chapter provides a unique perspective on how to look at finances both personally and for the home.

One of the things that our society doesn't do enough of is teach sound financial strategies. I believe that this should start in elementary school with basic accounting and personal finance classes. Kids should be taught budget-planning strategies at a young age. If we put as much emphasis on finances as we do about passing standardized tests, then our citizens wouldn't be in such a financial crisis. As I'm writing the opening to this chapter, I just Googled personal savings of Americans. The results show that 57% of Americans have less than $1,000 in their savings account.

Folks, if we don't get a grip on finances, debt, and strategies to grow wealth, then the disparity between the upper class and the lower class will continue to increase. Teach your kids at a young age the importance of financial responsibility.

The guests in this chapter offer great insight. Enjoy!

BEYOND THE MIC

Three Recommended Readings from Eric Verdi-

The Richest Man in Babylon by George Samuel Clason

Money by Tony Robbins

Bank On Yourself by Pamela Yellen

If you read one or all 3 of these books and put to work just one of the strategies, then you won't be in that 57% bracket.

HOME AND FINANCE

"Believe in Yourself."

MIKE HAGGERTY

BEYOND THE MIC

Episode #3 – Mike Haggerty – Lender/Mortgage Consultant – Presidential Bank Mortgage

Mike Haggerty

Mike Haggerty (Email: mhaggerty@presidential.com) has been in the mortgage industry for over 22 years. He is a lender and mortgage consultant with Presidential Bank Mortgage, but that's not where he started out. After college, he sold forms and business supplies to some of the larger corporations in the D.C. area. He transitioned in the real estate market while at the same time being a bartender. This unique combination presented a challenge as Mike had to balance late nights bartending and early mornings in real estate. It wasn't until a friend offered him an opportunity at Presidential that he made a full commitment to real estate.

Common Misconceptions About Home Loans

Being in the industry for so long, Mike has seen many changes in mortgages throughout the years. One of those changes is interest rates. As many of us know and have experienced, interest rates are significantly lower than they were 20 years ago. In fact, Mike mentioned that the highest interest rate he's seen was around 9.5 – 10.5%!

Given the fluctuations that come with interest rates, he has seen how those changes can prompt people to want to refinance. But he cautions that a drop in interest rates doesn't always mean that a homeowner should refinance. Instead, they should focus on the terms of the loan and overall monthly payment. Many people don't realize that property taxes can differ greatly from one area to another, which can make a difference in the total payment amount. A change in interest rates by a half a percent really won't make that much of a difference.

I also talked with Mike about how so many people feel that they need to save to put down 20% when they purchase a home. It's a common misconception that often discourages people from buying a home, but it doesn't have to be that way. The truth is that many products are available to help homebuyers with their financing. There are VA loans that provide 100% financing as well as conventional loans that require as little as 3.5% down.

Other factors do come into play as far as interest rates, such as your current situation and your credit score. Most loans favor those individuals who have a score of 640 or higher. Some loans may also charge mortgage insurance premiums or a one-time upfront fee, which can impact your interest rate as well.

Mike also recommends that people look beyond what the interest rate is if they are considering refinancing. In his business, he determines whether a homeowner should refinance on a case-by-case basis. If they only plan on staying in the house for a year or less, a refinance may not be worth it. If they have more long-term plans, refinancing could be a benefit. It's also important to note that the amount of equity in a home could also impact what course of action to take.

Believe in Yourself & Anything's Possible

One belief that is important to Mike, and it's one he instills in his children, is to believe in yourself. Once you do, there's nothing that can stop you. Sure, there may be roadblocks along the way, just believe. This motto actually helped him when a personal crisis struck. His mother fell ill, and the doctors gave her a very dismal chance of survival. Instead of giving up, he made a sign that said "Believe" and made sure she could see it from her bed. Eventually, her health was restored, and she now lives a very active life. It just follows through with Mike's belief that you should be able to accomplish any goal you set for yourself.

"The greatness of a nation and its moral progress can be judged by the way its animals are treated."
Gandhi

KATRINA HALLEIN

HOME AND FINANCE

Episode #4 – Katrina Hallein – Owner & Principal Agent at Lawyers Signature Settlements

Behind the Scenes of a Title - Katrina Hallein

Katrina Hallein (Email: katrina@signaturesettlements.com) is the owner and principal agent at Signature Settlements. She originally graduated from law school at the University of Baltimore with the intention of getting into estate planning. After an internship as a law clerk ended, a friend offered her a job at a title company. She worked there for a few years and then was approached by someone who wanted to sell her their title company. As her friend, I was able to go over the pros and cons of buying a settlement agency, and Katrina decided to move forward with the offer. She's now been the owner of the agency for over three years.

What Happens Between Signing a Contract on a Home & Closing?

Katrina is unique in that she strives to be personally involved in every contract that her firm handles. Not only does she want to know what's going on, but she wants her clients to know she's available. She's aware that the closing process can be stressful for some people. Actually, most people say that buying a home is more stressful than losing a job or a death in the family. This is specifically why she wants to make sure it's enjoyable happy experience for everyone involved.

So, what happens once someone signs a contract to purchase a home and closing?

The entire process takes about a month, and it involves several steps. First, Katrina reviews every single contract that comes through the door. It's important the tax statements are reviewed so that they can verify that it matches with the person who owns the home. Once that information is verified, a title is ordered.

A title will tell them everything that's been recorded in reference to the property. This includes any liens, judgments, or mortgage. A check is performed to ensure the title is clean and that the buyer won't experience any issues.

If the title is deemed to be clean, they issue a title insurance binder to the lender. This gives the lender an insurable security interest in the property. They then order homeowners' association fees and transfers of property to complete the process.

In the end, this entire series of steps is to ensure that the homebuyer is purchasing property that doesn't have any title issues. They won't have to worry about losing their home or end up in court due to any potential problems.

Fun Facts About Katrina

- Katrina grew up in Maine and moved to Maryland when she was 5.
- She grew up on a farm and spent many days and weekends helping her family with making hay and handling farm activities.
- She isn't required to be an attorney to be a settlement agent in Maryland but finds that her legal background aids in the process.
- Her firm handles settlements for both commercial and residential properties, including refinances, short sales, and foreclosures.

HOME AND FINANCE

"Under Promise and Over Deliver"

SHARI AULDRIDGE

BEYOND THE MIC

Episode #7 – Shari Auldridge – Owner – Staged Above

Insights on Home Staging & DIY Staging Tips

Shari Auldridge

If you ask Shari Auldridge (Email: shari@stagedabove.com URL: www.stagedabove.com) about how she got interested in the home staging business, she would tell you it all started when she was a kid! Her dad was in the military, so her family moved around a lot. Her mother loved to look at model homes wherever they were and she would take Shari along on the weekends or when she wasn't in school. She developed a love for it as well and knew it was something she wanted to do early on. Shari was a stay at home mom for twelve years before starting her business. She started off by decorating cakes, but quickly realized that it was a lot of work and it didn't pay off quite as well as she expected. It was when she left that venture that she decided to devote her time to opening and running her own staging business.

Shari's Insights on Home Staging and DIY Staging Tips

While there's no formal requirement to become a home stager, Shari is ASP® (Accredited Staging Professional) credited and she is a member of RESA® (Real Estate Staging Association). There are a lot of good courses someone can take if they're interested in joining the industry. It's also important to note that staging is much more than decorating. It takes training to be able to see what you do from a "buyer's eye" while not making them feel as if they're invading someone else's home.

Here are Shari's tips and insights on staging for your home:

- Your master bedroom and bathroom need to look like a 5-star hotel and spa. Shari's best suggestion is to go to a store like Target and buy big, fluffy white towels for the

bathroom. She's also happy to help if you need her to do the "hotel fold" on them.
- Don't overlook color. You can easily add more color to a room such as putting throw pillows on your couches.
- In your kitchen, leave only one or two appliances on the countertops. Put the rest away to avoid clutter.
- Do a Q-tip® clean. Make sure your home is spotless.
- Make sure rooms are put back to their purpose. For example, if you've been using your dining room as a playroom for the kids, clear away any toys so that it looks like an actual dining room again.
- Always remember that photos go together with staging. Before you call a realtor, view the room from the camera lens on your phone. Make sure the room looks good from perspective as a buyer can easily eliminate a choice based on photos alone.

Keep in mind that buyers want a move-in ready home. They don't want to have to worry about things being added to their "no list" as they walk through your home. They want to be assured that the home they buy won't require them to do a lot of things and by staging your home, you can avoid that from being a potential problem.

Under Promise and Over Deliver

Shari follows this motto throughout her role as a business owner. She's found, as many other entrepreneurs have, that if you over promise and under deliver, your customers are going to complain. Not to mention that just one unhappy customer can spread the word quickly through friends and social media. However, when you under promise and over deliver, you can keep people happy and keep those positive referrals working to grow your business.

"In the end, everything will be okay. If it's not okay, it's not the end." John Paul DeJoria

TERESA KUHN

HOME AND FINANCE

Episode #8 – Teresa Kuhn – Owner – Living Wealthy Financial Group

Wealth Building Strategies and Money Myths

Teresa Kuhn

Teresa Kuhn (URL: LivingWealthyFinancialGroup.com) is one of those people who was born an entrepreneur. She started working at the age of 16 and started working in securities when she was in college. She successfully went on to law school, and has practiced law in D.C., Virginia, and Maryland. When her husband was transferred to Ohio, she realized that given her background, she has limitless options to do what she wanted. It was here that Teresa had the opportunity to work with one of the biggest real estate developers in the area. That experience taught her the power of the entrepreneurial mindset, which was in direct contrast to that of a risk-adverse lawyer mindset. When she opened her own practice, that mindset led her to only wanting happy clients and providing them with strategies that actually work and do what they say they're going to do.

The Wealth Building Strategy to Include in Your Portfolio

It's not often that you meet one of your mentors by chance, but that's exactly how I met Teresa a few years ago. I make it a habit to consistently read and search for books on topics like self-help and personal finance. I had just finished reading *The Richest Man in Babylon* by George Samuel Clason and was looking for a new book to read during a trip to the library with my son. I came across one titled *Bank on Yourself: The Life-Changing Secret to Protecting Your Financial Future* by Pamela Yellen and decided to check it out. I really enjoyed the book and the main strategy discussed was something that was new to me. At the end, they give you the option to contact a financial advisor for a free consultation. And that's when I was first introduced to Teresa.

Teresa is one of a group of advisors throughout the country that follows the strategy Bank on Yourself®. It's a strategy that's been around for over one hundred years and it involves the use of a whole life insurance policy. When used as a financial vehicle, this specific type of policy can help individuals, families, and business owners build their financial house with a strong, rock-solid foundation, and without the risk that comes with other options available. It's designed to survive and increase in value no matter what happens with the economy, the stock market, or real estate. In fact, it's increased in value through every stock crash to provide people with financial peace.

A whole life insurance policy offers a cash value, which provides a policyholder with the option to borrow against it, withdraw funds, or just leave alone to grow in value. It's basically like having another bank account that you can utilize as you see fit. Business owners have used the funds to purchase equipment for their company. Individuals and families have used it to put a down payment on a home or make other large purchases like a wedding or a car.

It's important to note that Teresa's firm as well as others who follow this strategy have a unique way of designing their policies to provide this benefit. They've built in specific features and benefits so that from day one, your policy has cash value.

Money Myths to Avoid

Over the years, Teresa has seen a lot of myths about money that prevent people from building a more secure financial foundation.

Here are some of the most popular myths Teresa cautions her clients to avoid:

- Investing vs. Saving – with the recent economic downturn, we saw interest on savings account plummet. However, that doesn't mean that we should avoid saving. Many people think that it's not worth it to save at a 1% interest

rate, but they forget the fact that savings can get you through any crisis and it doesn't involve risk like investing does. While it's great to have money working for you, it's more important to have the stability a saving account can offer.
- Buy a term life insurance policy and invest the difference – If you're building up your savings and investing properly, by the time you retire, you likely won't need term life insurance. Teresa's clients have the assurance that their whole life insurance policy is growing, it's there when they need it, and it provides them with options for their future.
- Investing in Wall Street – while some would argue that the average investment grows 10-12% per year, it may not provide you with financial peace. Whether you agree with the numbers or not, the reality is that investing involves three core emotions: fear, greed, and exuberance. These are the exact emotions that guide someone when they gamble! They experience fear when the market goes down, greed when they've earned money, and exuberance when they see the market go up. The fact is that emotions rule investing. With safer financial vehicles, you're no longer worrying about what the market does, and you're not chasing after money, which leads you to become more grounded with money and develop financial peace.

"In the end, everything will be okay…"

Teresa had the opportunity to see John Paul DeJoria speak at a conference she attended. He talked about his hardships growing up and something he said resonated with her. "In the end, everything will be okay. If it's not okay, it's not the end." This quote stood out to her as it reflects what she believes about her clients and their financial success. She has seen this one thing stand out in those clients that are open to what's available to them. It's what she calls a "learning mindset." It's when people take the opportunity to read books and learn about all of their financial options that they can weather any storm and know that in the end, everything will be okay.

"Its not always the best to go with the cheapest policy."

SEAN QUILL

HOME AND FINANCE

Episode #10 – Sean Quill – Owner – Nationwide Insurance Agency Office in Frederick

Importance of Knowing Your Insurance Coverage

Sean Quill

Sean Quill (Email: quills2@nationwide.com) transitioned from a career in commercial banking into owning an insurance agency due to the recession. Around the same time that business started to drop, he was approached by the local Nationwide insurance agent who was getting ready to retire and needed someone to take over the agency. If it wasn't for the economic downturn, he admits that he may not have considered changing careers. He decided to take the leap, and it's worked out well for him. What some people may not know is that Sean is my cousin. Even though his degree is in Accounting and he worked in commercial banking for many years, he's embraced his new role as an insurance agent and business owner.

Why You Should Know What Insurance Coverage You Have & Don't Have

One thing that helps Sean stand out as an insurance agent is that he never stops trying to make a good impression. It's what keeps his current clients happy, and it's what helps him grow his business through referrals. He also does a lot for the community, which shows in his tenure as Board President of the Tourism Council of Frederick County. So, when it comes to serving clients new and old, he makes no exception.

As an insurance agent, he's happy to review existing policies to make sure that a person is covered adequately. A common mistake he sees among policyholders is buying coverage based on price. In reality, insurance is much more than just the monthly premium you pay. If you're focused solely on the amount of the premium, you could be setting yourself up for heartbreak in the future.

Some people are happy to make their insurance payment thinking they're covered. But that mindset can lead to a false sense of security if you're not educated on how much coverage you have. This is especially true with the limits that you have built-in to your policy. Limits are one of the main factors that decide the amount of your premium. If your limit is lower than the coverage you actually need, you will be responsible for the difference. For example, if your auto policy states that the limit is $15,000 for property damage liability and you're at fault in an accident that totals someone else's $40,000 car, that $25,000 difference is your responsibility.

The same philosophy stands for if you have a major fire in your home or someone gets hurt on your property and claims it's your fault. If the limits on your coverage aren't sufficient, you will have to find a way to make up the difference between the actual cost and what your insurance covers.

Another common mistake Sean sees is in purchasing coverage online or over the phone. While both options are convenient and will provide you with coverage, you may end up missing out on what's actually available to you. For instance, you may not realize that by just paying $50 more, you could possibly triple your coverage.

Sean enjoys spreading the word about insurance and educating people on why it's so important to have the right amount of coverage. Most agents are like him and are happy to go over your existing policies to review what coverage you have as well as any other options available to you. Always keep in mind that your insurance should cover what it costs to replace or rebuild property and you'll avoid financial heartache in the end.

HOME AND FINANCE

"There are no stupid mistakes, only lessons from the Universe."

DAMION LUPO

Episode #15 – Damion Lupo – Owner – My Gold Advisor

Benefits of Investing in Metals

Damion Lupo

Damion Lupo (http://www.mygoldadvisor.com/) grew up in Alaska but left shortly after his high school graduation to escape from such a remote location. He spent time all over the country and took part in over 30 businesses that fueled his entrepreneurial passions. It was when the economic downturn in 2008 hit that he stumbled across precious metals. Damion combined his knowledge with his passion for teaching to build his business, My Gold Advisor.

The Benefits of Investing in Precious Metals

Damion first got into precious metals because his dad was a coin collector. His dad had a second-hand store in Montana, so he was introduced to how precious metals like gold and silver can appreciate in value. When the 2008 financial crisis hit, Damion sold everything off and bought gold and silver because it was something everyone was talking about. He quickly realized that he could use this newfound knowledge to help others protect their investments.

One of the biggest benefits of investing in precious metals is that it gives people more control over what happens with their money. With stocks, you're left vulnerable to the whims of Wall Street. In other words, a company's actions can have a major impact on your portfolio. Their business could fail, their executives could commit fraud or participate in any other illegal act, and the result is your portfolio decreasing in value. You have no control over how the market is going to react, and it puts the money you've worked so hard for at risk.

Another benefit to investing in precious metals is that it gives you something physical to hold. You can safely store it in a way that you see fit, which also makes it easily accessible. You can also use a QRP (qualified retirement plan) account that gives you checkbook access to your retirement money, use it to purchase gold and silver, and have the metals delivered where you want it.

The main message that Damion shared with me is to avoid letting Wall Street from having control over your money. Having a hard asset like precious metals protects your investments, and you don't have to worry about what Wall Street is or isn't doing to affect your accounts. Precious metals always have the benefit that they don't have anything to manipulate it.

"There Are No Stupid Mistakes..."

When I asked Damian about a quote that resonates with him, he mentioned that "There are no stupid mistakes, only lessons from the universe that are gifts for us to grow." To him, this means that either we learn and evolve or the universe is going to send those lessons back to us in another form to repeat. We should always take advantage of our mistakes and learn from them so that we can grow and our lives continue to get better.

"Be truthful, gentle, and fearless." - Ghandi

WHITNEY CARPENTER

HOME AND FINANCE

Episode #26 – Whitney Carpenter – Owner – Billwood Properties

The Benefits of Investing in Turnkey Properties

Whitney Carpenter

Whitney Carpenter (URL: http://www.billwoodproperties.com/) grew up in Hagerstown, Maryland. After suffering a loss with her first venture into real estate investing, she quickly realized that she didn't have to risk everything by using a large sum of money to invest in property. She and her husband discovered a way to purchase property with only $25,000, and that's when everything fell into place. They built their income portfolio from there, and at first, their focus was on having a rental portfolio. With the growth they experienced, Billwood Properties was created as a property management company to handle more than 150 properties in their portfolio. Whitney is also the author of the book The Passive Way to Passive Income.

The Benefits of Investing in Turnkey Properties

Purchasing real estate can be overwhelming and stressful in any circumstance. As Whitney will attest to, many people make the mistake of thinking that they need a large amount of cash to get started. Actually, there are many strategies available where you can purchase properties at a cheap rate.

When you pick out a property that you want to purchase, in most cases, you have to use cash or hard money to finance the deal. When you the turnkey method, you have the ability to avoid using cash. In addition, the remodeling is already done, so you're able to use traditional financing.

By using a company like Billwood Properties, who already has the capacity to handle the renovations, you can avoid the hassle of having to manage a project or a team to handle it. You'll save time and prevent a lot of the stress and overwhelm that comes with renovating a property.

Renovating a property is just one piece that you can have outsourced, but then the next stage is actually renting the property. This stage can be a long and involved process that means sorting out tenants, doing background checks, running credit reports, and overall screening. Billwood Properties includes that as part of their services, so you can be worried about more important things like purchasing your next property.

Billwood Properties also offers property management services to the new owner of the property once it's sold. Having someone like them in your corner can help you to avoid the hardships of real estate investing and take away all the guesswork. There are a lot of unknowns, especially if you're first starting out, so it's good to have a resource to guide you through the process.

"There is no passion to be found in playing small - in settling for a life less than what you are capable of living." Nelson Mandela

---

JAMAAL RASHAD

Episode #37 – Jamaal Rashad – LegalShield

Four Reasons Why You Should Have Access to Legal Services

Jamaal Rashad

Jamaal Rashad (URL: www.jamaalrashad.com) moved to Virginia when he was 3 or 4 as his dad was in the military. When he first graduated from college, he went to work for UPS but wasn't happy with the working conditions. He actively sought out a part-time job, which was when he was introduced to LegalShield by someone at his gym in 2010. He left UPS in 2013 and has been helping people to secure legal services ever since.

Four Reasons Why You Should Have Access to Legal Services

Jamaal can't emphasize enough why people should have affordable and easy access to legal services. Whether you are in need of services for bankruptcy, divorce, or estate planning, a typical attorney will charge you $200-$300 per hour. But with a service like LegalShield, you pay a small monthly fee that grants you access to a qualified attorney as well as identity theft protection services. The attorneys in their database are chosen from the top providers in their state, and in most cases, they average being in business for fifteen years or more.

Some of Jamaal's prospective clients state that they already know an attorney or they're healthy and don't expect to die anytime soon. However, he says there are still four major reasons why you should have access to a service like LegalShield.

1. Access to a Proven System Used by a Majority of People – people who have access to this system have the ability to contact an attorney at any time. They have attorneys in their systems that cover all areas of the law. The service

HOME AND FINANCE

   also works if you're away from your local area or out of state when an issue arises.
2. Estate Planning – As Jamaal says, seven out of ten people don't have their will done, nine out of ten minorities don't have one, and nine out of ten single parents don't have one. But, ten out of ten people ***need*** one. All too often, he sees people procrastinate and think they're not going to die soon, but that can have dangerous consequences if something unexpected happens. They also offer living will and healthcare powers of attorney through their services.
3. Motor Vehicle Representation – If you get pulled over by police and they write you a ticket, you will want to fight it as it can have negative effects on your driving record and insurance rates. If you just pay the ticket, you admit guilt. And to show up in court can take precious time away from work and family. In most cases, LegalShield can send an attorney to court for you without you needing to be present to fight the ticket.
4. Identity Theft Protection – If your identity is stolen, the average time it takes to restore it is 500 hours. That is a significant amount of time that is taken away from your life for something that wasn't your fault. By having protection in place, you can minimize your chances of being a victim of this crime and having someone in your corner to help restore your good name.

"There is No Passion to be Found in Playing Small…"

Jamaal references the above quote by Nelson Mandela as one that's inspiring to him. He also points to the books, *Start with Why* by Simon Sinek and *The 10x Rule* by Grant Cardone as resources that have helped him be successful in business.

"Understand the Rules of the Money Game."

DARRICK BOWENS

Episode #51 – Darrick Bowens – Colbert Ball Franchise Owner

Giving Back by Turning a Dream into Reality

Darrick Bowens

Darrick Bowens (http://www.colbertballtax-frederick.com/) was born and raised in Frederick, Maryland. He was heavily into sports as a youth and played basketball, football, and baseball throughout high school. He played basketball in college but ended up changing directions and has spent most of his career in the insurance, finance, and tax accounting fields.

That change came when Darrick was in the military. He had his taxes done by someone and thought he was going to receive an $800 refund. Instead, he received a letter from the IRS stating that he owed $800. At that moment, he decided that he would do his own taxes from then on. He became a Colbert Ball franchisee and enjoys the support he gets from having a large corporation backing his business.

Giving Back by Turning a Dream into Reality

Darrick's quote in his high school yearbook was that wanted to be a business owner. He's always dreamed of being in business for himself, and it's what led him to where he is today. Through his business, he has the ability to teach people how to understand the rules of the money game. He can help others to create wealth and create a legacy for their family.

With his business, Darrick is also able to follow in his grandmother's legacy of giving. His grandmother was someone who was known in their neighborhood for making biscuits and rolls on Sundays and handing them out to members of the community.

For Darrick, the tax business not only has its own unique "season," but also has its ebbs and flows just like any other business. One time, he had a client come in early in the season to have her taxes done. He realized that due the brace on her wrist that she was having health issues. She also admitted to him that she needed her tax refund to pay for medical expenses and that she and her fiancée were getting married at the courthouse because they couldn't afford a wedding.

Darrick was in the habit of giving away vacation vouchers to select clients and knew one had to go to her. By giving her a honeymoon, not only did it impact her life, but it impacted him as well. He states that when a day doesn't go quite as expected, he refers back to that moment as a source of inspiration.

Selling Yourself and Your Business

Darrick cites the book *Go-Givers Sell More* by Bob Burg and John David Mann as one that he re-reads often. It reminds him that even though he's providing a service, he still has to sell himself as well as his business.

The book talks about the laws of influence, compensation, values, and authenticity. It also helps him to draw on his grandmother's inspiration, which shows in his work with non-profits where he often gives presentations on financially-related material.

HEALTH AND WELLNESS

HEALTH & WELLNESS

Good Health and Good Sense are life's two Greatest Blessings. –
Pubilius Syrus

Introduction – Health and Wellness

One of the largest segments of small business and entrepreneurs in the U.S. is the Health and Wellness sector. This played out in Frederick Advice Givers in exactly the same format. Some of the businesses are built on the MLM strategy, which is right for some people, but doesn't fit others. There are standalone businesses. There are family physicians. There are gym owners. There are rehab specialists. And there are nutritionists all featured in this section.

This section will have a profound effect on how you view your health and wellness going forward.

Like finances, there is not one specific strategy that will make you healthy. But diet and exercise are at the top of everyone's list in 'getting healthy.'

You will discover some great wellness strategies within this section. In fact, some of these strategies you may not have considered before. And then, you will be introduced to some entrepreneurs who will give you tips for health improvement whether you are in good health or you are looking to have better health.

My goal is that when you are done with this section you feel motived to go out there and do SOMETHING about your long-term health and wellness.

Enjoy!

"Dream Big"

AMY GOLDSMITH

HEALTH AND WELLNESS

Episode #5 – Amy Goldsmith - Dietician – Kindred Nutrition

Understanding the Difference Between a Nutritionist & a Dietician

Amy Goldsmith

Amy Goldsmith (URL: www.KindredNutrition.com) had many influences early in life to lead her down a path to becoming a dietician. As a child, her younger brother had severe food allergies, which caused her mother to hire a nutritionist. When she was younger, her dad had bladder cancer for a period of time. It was when encyclopedias were popular, so she used them to read up on carcinogens. She was also an athlete in track and soccer, so nutrition was always important to her. After graduating from college, fulfilling her internship, and doing some traveling, Amy became a Clinical Dietician at John Hopkins. She left there after a year and a half, to work at an oncologist wing at Washington Hospital Center and then after obtaining the clinical training she needed focused on product development and sales management and development in the corporate world. For the last eight years, she's run her own business, Kindred Nutrition.

What's the Difference Between Nutritionists and Dieticians?

Many people, myself included, don't understand the difference between a nutritionist and a dietician. When I asked Amy to clarify, she told me that nutritionists aren't as regulated as some might think.

A nutritionist can take continued education courses or tests online to achieve the knowledge to practice in their field. There is no minimum education and no annual regulation or licensure. While the requirements aren't as strict, most nutritionists are passionate about their profession and are dedicated to helping their clients.

Dieticians are required to go through a 4-year Didactic Program in Dietetics where they learn more detailed subject matter such as chemistry and anatomy. Once they graduate, they are required to obtain 750 – 1,000 hours of internship, which usually works out to a year's time. After that, they are eligible to take a registration exam. Once they pass, they are required to accumulate 75 hours of continued education every five years or their registration is revoked. Most also have to abide by their state licensure which is tightly regulated.

One point that Amy emphasized to me was that dieticians do much more than just prescribe meal plans. They are actually an important part of your medical team as they can request and assess labs, recommend supplementation when there are deficiencies, and work with your physician to recommend further evaluation during the diagnostic phase of treatment. Their work is much more involved in that they are trained and licensed to provide individualize treatments for every client and various diagnosis'. They also teach people how to prepare food in a healthy way to help them reach a specific goal.

Her philosophy is that it's not about good food or bad food. It's more about what a person eats in an entire day. Through her work, she helps a wide variety of people from those who want help weight management, sports nutrition, disease prevention or treatment, or eating disorders.

One case stands out for Amy, and she told me that talking about it gives her goosebumps. A client came to her who had been diagnosed as morbidly obese, and her doctor recommended a gastric bypass. She was also pre-diabetic and at risk for other serious health problems. When she came to Amy, she wanted to know if it was possible for her health to improve. She was very dedicated to improving her health and losing weight. She worked with Amy on her nutrition for 6 months when she got to a point where she could safely exercise. Once able, she worked out three times a week. After about nine months, her patient weighed in at 97 pounds less than her original visit.

That story is important to Amy not only because of her client's success but also because it shows that accountability for yourself and your goals can be a major difference in your results.

A Realist with Big Dreams

Amy referenced Steve Jobs' biography when I asked her about things that have been a positive influence in her life. She admitted she reads it once a year because it really speaks to her. Even though she knows that not everyone may be a fan of Steve Jobs as a person, the book is important to her because of his vision and ability to brand. It's actually a favorite book of mine too.

Amy describes herself as "realist with big dreams." At the closing part of our interview, she mentioned that if you don't dream big, you'll never know what you're going to be able to achieve.

"Deeds, and not words, are what count most"
Napoleon Hill

ALEENA STEELE

HEALTH AND WELLNESS

Episode #12 – Aleena Steele - Wellness Advocate – doTerra Essential Oils

Insights About the Health Benefits of Essential Oils

Aleena Steele

Aleena Steele (URL: https://www.facebook.com/essentialoilswithaleenasteele/ Email: doTerraOilsWithAleena@gmail.com) is originally from Louisiana but has lived in Frederick, Maryland since 2002. She was a certified pharmacy technician for twelve years, so she had a healthcare background before venturing into the world of essential oils. Aleena admits that she was just as skeptical as most people are when introduced to essential oils. She was so used to seeing how prescription and over the counter medicine benefitted patients that essential oils sounded too good to be true. But once she saw the benefits to her family's health, she couldn't ignore the evidence. What has really impressed her is that the oils empower people to have control over their health. They provide another option for managing health and made her realize that drugs aren't always the only option.

The Health Benefits of Essential Oils

When synthetic drugs are used, side effects can occur as they are man-made and not a natural substance. Many people may not understand that our bodies recognize plant materials due to our chemistry, which makes essential oils very useful.

Essential oils can be used in three ways:

- Aromatically – through aromatherapy or with the use of a diffuser
- Topically – the oils can be applied directly to the skin
- Internally – oils that are CPTG, Certified Pure Therapeutic Grade can be ingested

The type of oil and how it is used will depend on what ailment you're trying to treat or prevent. What some may find interesting is that when it's applied topically, the soles of the feet are ideal. There are a few reasons for this. With those of us with sensitive skin, like young children, the bottom of the feet is a less sensitive area of the body. Our feet have the most pores per square inch on our bodies. This allows the essential oils to be absorbed very quickly. REFLEXOLOGY! The bottoms of our feet are directly connected to the rest of our body.

Aleena stresses that it's important to use essential oils that are pure and of high-grade quality. doTerra participates in third-party testing to ensure the highest quality. They also source the plants that provide the oils from where the oils grow natively and abundantly. Co-Impact Sourcing™ by doTERRA helps health-conscious individuals find safe alternatives while also lifting entire communities and giving them a hope for the future. As part doTERRA's promise to provide pure, potent, consistent essential oils, Co-Impact Sourcing ensures that the doTERRA CPTG Certified Pure Therapeutic Grade® process starts at the source. For instance, lavender is native to France, so that's where their lavender oil is obtained from. It ensures quality as their source knows the condition of the plants from start to finish. They've been in business from generation to generation and therefore, can harvest and distill the plants at the highest possible quality.

Aleena and her family use essential oils to support their bodies and emotions for a wide range of ailments. Whether she's dealing with seasonal threats or her kids have a little tummy trouble, there's an essential oil to provide support.

HEALTH AND WELLNESS

"Word Spreads when you take Care of your Patients"

DR. JULIO MENOCAL

BEYOND THE MIC

Episode #13 – Dr. Menocal – Family Practitioner – Menocal Family Practice

How Personal Connections Build a Successful Business

Dr. Menocal (URL: http://www.menocalfamilypractice.com/) is originally from Cuba. His family emigrated from there in 1961 after the revolution and settled here in the U.S. He went on to live in Mexico and Colombia, where he went to medical school. He eventually came back to the U.S. with a residency in Georgetown, and now has his practice in three locations across the Frederick, Maryland area.

Using Personal Connections to Grow a Successful Business

Dr. Menocal has been a board-certified family practitioner for over 30 years. He took over his current practice from two doctors and has centered it around serving a diverse set of patients. One thing that grabbed his attention was when Frederick County experienced an influx of the Hispanic community in 2006. This group of people were largely undocumented and had children who hadn't been vaccinated. He then built his practice around serving this community and catering to their needs, and had major success in improving vaccination rates.

Even though the emphasis was on being a specialist when he was in medical school in the '70s, he wanted to be a family practitioner. He realized that there was a disconnect between what the patient needed and what the patient was receiving care for. There never seemed to be someone available for them to go to for their individual needs, and he wanted to change that. Now, he has helped literally generations of families. He's seen my grandmother, mother, myself, and my kids as patients, and has even mentioned that he'd like to be around to provide care for my future grandchildren!

HEALTH AND WELLNESS

Not only is his longevity impressive, but it's in his personal connections that have made his practice so successful. In fact, some of his patients have commented that he doesn't need to look at their chart when they go in for a visit, as he already knows their medical history. I've always appreciated how Dr. Menocal is willing to go the extra mile, run tests or investigate what's going on with his patients. He believes that no matter what's going on with a patient and their personal situation, it is always important to focus on their health and well-being.

It's no surprise that Dr. Menocal has fun and enjoys what he does. He takes personal ownership in his practice and in doing so, befriends those within his community and sees his patients grow up and have their own families. One of his main goals is to get people to listen when it comes to preventative medicine. While it's difficult to convince people to have routine check-ups and testing done, it can be rewarding when they see it's a good thing to do.

Dr. Menocal's attitude towards his patients reflects in the success of his practice and how his patient's respect him. Even though he's changed the way the underserved population is taken care of, he is happy to see all members of his community.

"True perfection is unattainable, but if you chase perfection, you will catch excellence." Vince Lombardi

---

LEE ANDERSON

HEALTH AND WELLNESS

Episode #14 – Lee Anderson – Owner – Kicks Karate

The Five Benefits of Karate

Lee Anderson

It might be surprising to some that Lee Anderson (URL: http://kickskarate.com/) got into karate purely by accident. It all started when he was 8, and his mom missed all the summer camp registration deadlines. His parents both decided that he needed to participate in some activity for the summer but were at a loss as to what it would be. It wasn't until a neighborhood kid walked by the house in his karate uniform that it became apparent. His mom tracked down the kid and found out where he was taking lessons so that she could enroll Lee. And all because of that introductory lesson, Lee discovered a passion that carried over into his adult life.

The Five Benefits of Karate

Even though martial arts become a passion for Lee, it wasn't always his priority. He did well with martial arts and as an intern to assist class instructors; eventually, Lee wanted to put aside karate to try soccer. He went to practice, but after a few scrimmages, he was cut from the team. So, as fate would have it, he turned back to karate and has been there ever since.

When kids come into the school, he sees and hears a lot of reasons for why they want to sign up. Regardless of their physical skills or mental abilities, five main benefits apply to how karate can impact your life.

1. Stimulates both physical and mental attributes at the same time
2. Boosts self-confidence
3. Improves self-discipline
4. Provides a learning opportunity in a fun way

5. Gives a sense of accomplishment

It's easy to see how all of these can positively impact someone, especially a child. This was especially the case when Lee once helped a child who had Down's Syndrome. It can often be difficult for kids with this condition to do their form let alone in front of others. When the school does black belt testing, it's done as a group in front of other students, parents, and instructors. Not only did this one child do his form accurately but he did it in front of everyone and he nailed it! Lee and his fellow instructors felt a strong sense of pride because their work helped one of their students in a large and unexpected way.

"True Perfection is Unattainable…"

Lee has always been a believer in hard work and dedication. So, it's no surprise that a quote by Vince Lombardi is so important to him. "True perfection is unattainable, but if you chase perfection, you will catch excellence."

Lee sees a lot of people sign-up for karate lessons. Some stay for a while, some end up quitting, but there's also a group of people who feel like it's too late for them to start. Lee's message to them is that it's never too late to start. Regardless of your reason for wanting to start, you're never too old to do what's important to you or to take care of yourself.

HEALTH AND WELLNESS

"A ship in the harbor is safe, but that is not what ships are for." John Augustus Shedd

---

STACY ALLGOOD-SMITH

BEYOND THE MIC

Episode #17 – Stacy Allgood-Smith – Owner – Allgood Therapeutic Massage

The Benefits of Massage Therapy

Stacy Allgood-Smith

Stacy Allgood-Smith (URL: http://www.allgoodmassage.com/) didn't originally start out to become a massage therapist. But her journey led her down a path that is nothing short of an epiphany. She is a self-proclaimed "music geek" and worked for a pension fund for 18 years, at least until the financial crisis in 2009. Stacy was laid off and faced with settling for a data entry job because that's all that was available. That circumstance combined with significant deaths in the family sent her into depression. When her family went on a much-needed vacation in Florida shortly after, Stacy decided to treat herself to a massage, and her life was forever changed.

After the massage, she got up from the table and realized how amazing she felt in spite of her recent struggles with depression. It was then that she knew she wanted to do the same to help others feel amazing. And six weeks later, she was in massage school! It was a struggle at first as she worked forty hours a week at her regular job and went to school four nights a week in addition to several weeks in clinic on Saturdays. She kept going though, as she knew that her short-term sacrifice would lead to fulfilling a long-term goal.

The Benefits of Massage Therapy

Stacy loves the fact that she can use her hands in a compassionate to work the muscles as well as provide benefits to the skin. But what many may not realize is that massage therapy can provide a number of other benefits to people on both an emotional and physical level.

While massage therapy can relieve pain and discomfort, it also increases blood flow and circulation. This will aid in the removal of metabolic waste, toxins, and impurities within the body. Not only will this help you have a healthier body, but it will also help the body work properly and potentially lower blood pressure.

Massage therapy can often trigger an emotional reaction in a person. The muscles can carry an emotion, which when massaged, can release and create a response. When this happens, Stacy shows compassion and helps her clients work through the emotion and assures them that they're in a safe place and that it's a perfectly natural experience.

Some medications can create inhibitions in the muscles where a massage can help keep the muscles more pliable for ease of movement. A massage also helps with the release of endorphins, which is the body's natural painkiller. This release can also create a feeling of euphoria that can last as long as 48 hours, so it's no wonder that we feel so good after a massage!

In American society, it's no secret that we're stressed. It's just our culture to not take time for ourselves. This leads to the overproduction of cortisol, which creates the flight or fight response. When this is going on, all the secondary functions within the body, like digestion, will shut down. Having a massage produces a calm and relaxed state, which will significantly reduce stress and in turn lower cortisol levels for better health.

"A Ship in the Harbor is Safe…"

Stacy told me that there are two quotes that have inspired her on her journey to entrepreneurship. The first is one that I hadn't heard but also liked very much is by John Augustus Shedd: "A ship is safe in the harbor, but that's not what ships are for."

The other is one from Golda Meier: "Those who do not know how to weep with their whole heart don't know how to laugh either." Both of these are great quotes and reflect on those of us who may have struggled as we started our business but kept going and made it a success.

HEALTH AND WELLNESS

"Success Loves Speed"

DANI BURKHEAD

BEYOND THE MIC

Episode #20 – Dani Burkhead – Distributor – It Works Global

Helping Others Take Control of Their Health & Fitness

Dani Burkhead

Like most of the entrepreneurs I've talked to, Dani Burkhead (URL: www.danielleburkhead.com) got into her current business, It Works Global, by accident. She was always involved in business and had started her first company at the age of 22. When her husband suffered a traumatic injury playing soccer, it turned things upside down for their family. Suddenly, they were forced with trying to figure out how to pay the bills when he wasn't able to work. She saw someone post about It Works Global on social media. Although, she wasn't sure about it, she tried it anyway. She quickly experienced how it became a catalyst for amazing life changes in both her family's life and health.

A Tool to Consider Adding to Your Health & Wellness Plan

Even though the work Dani does can benefit someone's health, it isn't what's traditionally considered as part of a health and wellness plan. Yet, it's something she feels that people should look into as part of their self-care routine, which can lead to improved health and wellness.

For Dani, it's been a gift to see how through the products she sells that she can touch other people's lives. In one case, she was able to use their signature product, which is a body wrap designed to tighten and tone, to help someone reduce excess skin after a major weight loss. Instead of having to pay for an expensive procedure, her client was able to further boost her confidence by looking great after such a wonderful accomplishment.

Dani makes sure that people know that the It Global Works line has over 30 products to help with increasing energy, boosting weight loss efforts, and aid with sleep issues all without the use of harmful chemicals or additives. While people using the products won't experience benefits overnight, the entire line provides affordable, sustainable health benefits. They can be used as tools to help you stay motivated and keep going towards any health goal you're trying to achieve.

But Dani's business doesn't just help people with their health and wellness. As she personally experienced, It Works Global can also help people kindle their entrepreneurial spirit. In addition to her own success, she's seen a lot of lives change. With this type of business venture, people can turn a passion into a way to make money and provide for their family.

Favorite Resource for Inspiration

The Compound Effect by Darren Hardy is a book that Dani's read at least a dozen times, and it's one that she refers to often. It's about the concept of how small changes consistently over time can yield big results. You can be a dreamer, but if you don't put action behind it, they will stay dreams. It's also the last book I read before I hired an assistant and it provided me with the motivation to achieve greater goals in both my life and my business.

"Put your Oxygen Mask on First"

CHERYLE MCKEE

HEALTH AND WELLNESS

Episode #28 – Cheryle McKee – Nutritionist

How Working with a Nutritionist Can Improve Your Health

Cheryle McKee

Initially, Cheryle McKee (https://www.nourishingabundance.com/) wanted to be a doctor after watching a live birth on a TV after school special. Since she knew the cost was too high to go to med school, she discovered that programming was a high-paying field. She enrolled in DeVry, got a job, and ended up loving programming. She was in that career for 25 years but wanted to be there for her kids too. After juggling long hours and trying to be present at her kids' special events, she got rundown. One of her daughters also had minor ailments that needed to be addressed.

After being told that her daughter was too young for tests, Cheryle decided to start her on an elimination diet. Her ailments started to go away with the elimination of dairy and gluten. However, Cheryle was dealing with her own health issues, but the doctors couldn't find anything wrong. It wasn't until she started doing her own research into nutrition that she was able to find answers for her and her daughter.

How Working with a Nutritionist Can Improve Your Health

Given the amount of research Cheryle was doing, it wasn't long before other people started coming to her for advice. When someone recommended that she become a nutritionist, she went back to school and got her Master's degree while she worked her FT job. She was also required to do an internship, pass board exams, and get licensed.

Cheryle loves working with food and helping people to work on their wellness goals through nutrition to avoid getting sick. Although, most people that come to her are already sick and they look to her as a way to get better. One of her clients had Lyme Disease, lost her job, and was struggling to make ends meet. Due to her condition, it was important that she eat organic food in a simple, hassle-free way. Cheryle was able to create a plan for her that involved shopping at Whole Foods for only $60 per week. The plan included recipes that were simple and had minimal ingredients. Her patient started to improve and checked in with her regularly to tell her how Cheryle helped her to get better.

One thing that Cheryle thinks everyone should know is that 80% of your immune system is in your gut. If you're having digestive issues, you may be on the verge of getting sick. If it isn't remedied, your gut stays inflamed, which causes it to be leaky. Once this happens, any undigested food can seep into the body, which can lead to any of the various autoimmune diseases.

Another factor that can cause digestive issues is stress. It's important for Cheryle to show her clients how to balance stress and keep the immune system healthy. She also educates them on why it's important to eat real foods, avoid processed foods, get adequate sleep, exercise, and hydration.

Cheryle works directly with her clients to give them practical skills on healing and maintaining their health. She shows them how to shop for food, read nutrition labels, and how to cook the food in a healthy way. The one myth she wants to debunk is that her recommendations go well beyond "rabbit food." The suggestions she provides can help to keep you out of the drive-thru while being able to prepare food that your entire family can enjoy.

"Put Your Oxygen Mask on First"

If you've ever been on a plane, you know that every time you take off, you have to go through the ritual of being told what to do in case something goes wrong. For Cheryle, those procedures can also apply to us in our personal lives.

HEALTH AND WELLNESS

The flight attendants tell us to always put our own oxygen mask on first, and then you can assist another passenger with putting theirs on. We get so busy giving to everybody else, that it's an important reminder that we need to take care of ourselves. Some people may not feel worthy, so instead, they focus on their kids or spouse.

But Cheryle has to constantly tell her patients that they are worthy. Life is a gift, and we have to take care of that gift. It's not selfish to take care of ourselves. Keep in mind that when you feel good, you show up well too.

"Can you imagine what I would do if I could do all that I can?" Sun Tzu

DR. CRAIG HAUSER

HEALTH AND WELLNESS

Episode #33 – Dr. Craig Hauser – Functional Medicine Doctor

The Five Pillars of Functional Medicine

Dr. Craig Hauser

Dr. Craig Hauser (http://www.hauserhealth.com/) grew up in Colorado near the foothills by the Air Force Academy. It's where he developed his interests in science and medicine, which led to his career as a doctor. He went to school at Tulane University in New Orleans and served as an EMT for both the school and the city. After college, he went to med school through the Air Force and went into an internship. He had the unique opportunity to serve in bases and hospitals around the world. He also served as the Pacific Air Force's Consultant to the Surgeon General.

It was when he started having a long list of his own health troubles that he started to research alternative forms of medicine. After a medicine cabinet filled with prescription medicine resulted in him only getting sicker, he realized he needed something different. Dr. Hauser studied Chinese and Indian medicine, deep tissue massage, herbal remedies and supplements, acupuncture, and counseling. He first worked on his nutrition and exercise regime and went to counseling to help find ways to reduce stress. He was able to eventually get rid of the prescriptions and slowly started to feel better.

The Five Pillars of Functional Medicine

Dr. Hauser's personal journey of fighting illness helped him to fall in love with functional medicine. He realized that with it he could also help others. He decided to leave his job to open up his own practice, where he changed his specialty to an Integrative/Functional medicine doctor. He now has a special insight into his patients' health due to his own issues.

In the United States, the healthcare system is focused on Western medicine. This type of medicine is heavily focused on prescription drugs that often consist of dangerous side effects. The World Health Organization (WHO) ranked the U.S. as 37th of countries with the best healthcare. This low ranking reflects the fact that while we may spend a lot of money on healthcare, we also don't get great results.

With functional medicine, Dr. Hauser believes that you can combine the best of both worlds. He also shared with me the five pillars of functional medicine.

- Nutrition - we should be eating three healthy meals and two healthy snacks a day. The focus should be on quality proteins and fats while reducing or eliminating unhealthy grains and sugars. We should also eat plenty of fruits and vegetables and stay hydrated throughout the day.
- Sleep – everyone should aim to get at least seven to eight hours of sleep every night. Set yourself up for success with sleep hygiene that includes eliminating light, a room temperature of 68 degrees or lower, and removing electronic devices from the area where you sleep to avoid distractions.
- Exercise – we should move our bodies every day, but the exercise doesn't have to be strenuous. It can be as simple as taking the dog for a walk or having an evening walk every night with your family.
- Social – most of us don't put enough work into being happy. We should be incorporating more happiness, peace, and contentment in our daily lives.
- Nutraceuticals – eating the right foods isn't enough to provide our bodies with the correct level of nutrients due to depleted farm soils. We should be supplementing our diet with high-quality multivitamins, fish or cod liver oil, and a good probiotic.

HEALTH AND WELLNESS

The main distinction between Western medicine and functional/integrative medicine is that the focus is on getting to the root of disease for optimal results and healing.

"Practice, practice, all is coming" Sri K. Pattabhi

JULIE MELTON

HEALTH AND WELLNESS

Episode #35 – Julie Melton – Yoga Instructor

The Benefits of Yoga

Julie Melton

With a career in teaching elementary teaching, Julie Melton (https://juliemeltonyoga.com/) never envisioned that she would end up as a yoga instructor. In fact, she never really considered herself to be very flexible! When she was in college, she took a functional fitness class where she fell in love with running. When she trained for the Marine Corps marathon, she incorporated yoga as part of her training regime and never suffered an injury. When Julie attempted a triathlon next, she didn't stretch or utilize yoga technique and was banged up as a result. It was then that she investigated yoga as a discipline.

The Benefits of Yoga

Julie had her own firsthand experience with how yoga can be beneficial, especially for athletes. But there's more to yoga than just movement.

While yoga has proven to help people avoid injury, it also works to build strength to support your body. Julie looks at yoga as a form of pre-rehabilitation. If you can incorporate it into your life on a weekly basis, you'll gain flexibility and reduce your chances of getting injured.

Yoga can also act as a way to build confidence and vitality. By forcing you to focus on a specific movement or position, it gives you the ability to not panic in stressful situations. You're forced to focus on breathing and concentration to get oxygen in your body. This prepares you to tap into your innate ability to stay calm, figure out a situation so that you can handle it better.

Julie also stresses that yoga has a strong benefit for every person. If you take the time to seek out the right class to fit your needs, you will discover happiness, strength, reduced stress, and improved sleep. She points to a situation where a student was struggling with her knees and wasn't sure if she could do yoga. Julie worked with her to strengthen her muscles, and she was able to finish the class without her knees hurting. It's a great source of inspiration for her to know that she can use her studies to help other people.

Yoga Isn't About Being Perfect

Julie's favorite quote is "Practice, practice, all is coming," by the late Indian yoga teacher Sri K. Pattabhi. She states that many of her students get so focused on doing things perfectly, but that's not what yoga is about. It's really about doing the work that's in front of you. When you trust that, you'll know what to do next. Julie tells her students to trust and have faith that it's coming along the way.

"We have the power to influence those around us, whether for good or bad."

KATELYN LAFLIN

BEYOND THE MIC

Episode #43 – Katelyn Laflin – Wellness Educator at Juice Plus+

Why Fruits and Vegetables are Essential to Our Health

Katelyn Laflin

At a young age, Katelyn Laflin (URL: http://laflin.juiceplus.com) knew she had two passions. One was for helping people and the other was for food. Thankfully, she was able to find a career that is the perfect combination of the two! She graduated from the University of Denver with a degree in Hospitality Management and immediately started working in the restaurant business.

A hectic schedule with little sleep and eating only when she had a free moment made her realize that she wasn't quite as healthy as she thought she was. With a husband who had a background in Exercise Science and who went through Chiropractor school, she knew she had to turn things around and make her health a priority. Everything changed when a friend introduced her to Juice Plus+, where not only the product made sense but the business side was something she couldn't pass up due to her passions.

Why Fruits and Vegetables are Essential to Our Health

We've all heard that we're supposed to eat a recommended amount of fruits and vegetables every day. But, most of us also know that it's sometimes easier said than done.

That's why Katelyn feels so strongly about being a Wellness Educator with Juice Plus+. The company takes vine-ripened fruits and vegetables that are picked, juiced, and dried at low temperatures. They are then put into a capsule or chewable form for human consumption. It makes for a more convenient and affordable way to bridge the gap between the recommended 9 – 13 servings of fruits and vegetables a day we're supposed to eat and what we actually eat.

Even for people who are willing and able to consume that many servings, science is proving that the produce we buy doesn't carry the same level of nutrients that it used to. This means that we need to consume even more of it to get the full benefits.

As our body ages, it goes through a process called oxidative stress, which causes aging, disease, and cell damage. The only way for us to combat this is with antioxidants, which are found in fruits and vegetables. And if you think a multi-vitamin or supplement will do the trick, you may be doing more harm than good because it's made with synthetic ingredients that are difficult for your body to recognize. Supplements that are made from real food like Juice Plus+ are easy for your body to absorb since it's from a recognizable source.

Increasing your antioxidant intake from fruits and vegetables has shown to improve the immune system, reduce inflammation, reduce oxidative stress, and also help you to maintain a healthy DNA.

"...The Power to Influence Those Around Us..."

Katelyn states that the quote, "We have the power to influence those around us whether for good or bad," is very important to her. She considers it a way for people to challenge themselves to make an impact in their world for good.

"I do not understand the mystery of grace. Only that it meets us where we are, but does not leave us where it found us." Ann Lamont

---

SHABNAM SAMUEL

HEALTH AND WELLNESS

Episode #44 – Shabnam Samuel – Panchgani Writer's Retreat

Using Writing as a Way to Heal

Shabnam Samuel

Shabnam Samuel (http://www.panchganiwritersretreat.com/) grew up in India in the 1960s. One thing she takes away from that experience is that living in a biracial home was a privilege. With an Indian father and a Russian mother, she was taught from early on to be accepting and view everyone first as a human being. In her household, there was no discrimination due to race, religion, or culture because of her own diverse background.

Using Writing as a Way to Heal

Shabnam originally started out in business development in a large corporate setting. However, she gave it up to work on writing, which was her passion. For her, writing was about healing herself, and she wanted to help other women like her who had a strong story to tell. This desire led her to start her own event, Panchgani Writers Retreat, with a circle of friends who wanted to do something similar.

Shabnam's retreat is an annual event held in India, but it's about much more than writing. The message taught there is that writing is about healing and reaching out to others. Words can bring people together, but they also separate them. Since her retreat is in another country, it can be a challenge for different cultures to mesh. That's where words can be used to heal and to remove cross-culture borders.

The retreat is designed to give people the tools they need to write, but the event is also largely about mindfulness and wellness. Shabnam has also incorporated yoga, meditation, as well as Ayurvedic medicine, which is the world's oldest holistic healing system. While some may not view these aspects as essential to writing, they actually help people work towards a healthy life balance. The foods you eat and your state of mind can have a significant impact on your ability to write.

These tactics also help people with their creative synergy. Attendees of the retreat start the day with yoga and meditation and then can go to creative workshops in the poetry, fiction, and non-fiction categories. Their daily needs such as meals and laundry are taken care of for them, so the sole focus is on improving their writing skills.

The Role of Grace in Our Lives

Shabnam points to a quote by author Ann Lamont as one that's inspiring to her. "I do not understand the mystery of grace. Only that it meets us where we are, but does not leave us where it found us."

Grace is something she's grateful for even though she doesn't understand how it all works, and she doesn't profess to be religious. But she does know that grace is a big factor in one's life.

HEALTH AND WELLNESS

"Every human being is the author of their health."
Buddha

DR. ASHLEY RUSSELL

Episode #47 – Dr. Ashley Russell – Serenity Natural Health Center

Six Benefits of Naturopathic Medicine

Dr. Ashley Russell

Growing up in California, it's easy to see how Dr. Ashley Russell (http://serenitynhc.com/) was originally interested in the arts. Yet, she was also interested in the science which led her to get a degree in Applied Ecology with a focus on environmental concerns.

Her ailments as a child started her down the path she's on now. She suffered from major depression, went to counselors, and nothing worked. At a young age, she was put on a long list of medications that only increased as a teen due to additional health issues. She was also told that she would be on those medications for the rest of her life, which caused her to seek alternative options. It was her focus on nutrition that created positive results, and she was able to drastically reduce her medications. Discovering her own solutions made her want to pursue the field of Naturopathic medicine.

The Benefits of Naturopathic Medicine

Most people are unfamiliar with what a naturopathic doctor does. Here, Dr. Ashley explains the benefits of what she does and how it impacts her patients.

1. A naturopathic doctor is more like a health detective. They work to put all the pieces together to figure out the cause of what's going on with their patients.
2. Unlike traditional medicine, they give their patients options for their healthcare. Their patients aren't limited to just one solution.
3. Naturopathic medicine involves shared decision-making. In other words, she doesn't dictate to her patients. She

works together with them to make the decisions that affect their lifestyle, which is also why she encourages people to be honest about the issues they're having.
4. Instead of a quick appointment, Dr. Ashley spends 90 minutes with her patients on their first visit. It's important for her to learn about her patient's history, so she's better able to put on her "health detective" hat. It also helps to build better relationships with her patients.
5. Every treatment is individualized to the patient and their specific needs.
6. In Latin, the word "doctor" means "to teach." For Dr. Ashley, this means that a doctor is supposed to teach and empower their patient. A doctor should explain to the patient what's going on with them, so they are able to make things better.

Even though Dr. Ashley is focused on Naturopathic medicine, she believes that there is room for traditional medicine as well. When someone's in an accident or has a broken bone, traditional medicine and science have worked well to help people recover and feel better in those situations.

The Power to Be in Charge of Our Health

Dr. Ashley refers to Buddha's quote, "Every human being is the author of their health." It was a friend who pointed out the fact that every one of us has the power to change and take care of our health.

"To Help. To Heal. To Guide."

SARAH MARTUCCI

HEALTH AND WELLNESS

Episode #49 – Sarah Martucci – Medium, Crystal Healer, Jewelry Designer

Finding Healing and Guidance with a Medium

Sarah Martucci

Sarah Martucci (https://sarahmartucci.com/) grew up in Maryland, but as a medium, her childhood had awkward moments. Her ability to see the future of things and feel what other people were feeling without them saying anything got her labeled as a weird kid. But Sarah doesn't see this as a negative experience. It's what taught her to be strong, stand on her own two feet, and be sure of who she is.

Being born a medium, Sarah often felt the need to tap down her experiences, which would cause them to bubble out of her without warning. When she suffered from issues with her neck and was put in a brace for three months, she was forced to face a lot of truths about herself. She wasn't happy with her work or where she was in her life. She spoke with a therapist to confirm that the thoughts she was experiencing weren't crazy and she was able to confirm her calling. Now, Sarah is also a Certified Crystal Healer and makes jewelry.

Finding Healing and Guidance with a Medium

Sarah is constantly faced with people who have misconceptions about what a medium is. She's heard it all from people who think she's working with evil forces or that she's taking advantage of people. But Sarah stresses that this isn't what mediumship is about. It's more about helping people and offering guidance.

Seeing a medium can be helpful if you're trying to make a decision or get validation on a choice you're considering. It can also help you make a connection with a loved one who has passed. Or, you can also uncover the root of a problem you've been experiencing, and get help solving it.

With her added experience as a Certified Crystal Healer, Sarah can also recommend gems and stones for different aspects of your life, and she often incorporates them into her jewelry. While it may seem strange or weird, gems, stones, and rocks do have an energy to them. For business owners, she says there are three specific stones for prosperity. Malachite, citrine, and green aventurine are great to put near the front door of your business, or near a cash register. And if you work from home, they will also work if you place them close to your computer. The bigger the stone, the better.

Sarah says that people think she's crazy when she tells them to talk to the stones or crystals and tell them what you want. If you treat them like a sacred talisman, they will act in that way. Even if you don't believe in the metaphysical properties within the stones, you can still use them as a physical representation of what you want.

Take Action on What You Want to Do

Sarah points to a quote that has meant different things to her throughout different areas of her life. "It's better to light one candle than to curse the darkness," is a quote that has been attributed to many people including Eleanor Roosevelt and John F. Kennedy. For Sarah, it represents not complaining about what you can't do and taking action on what you want to do. It's been a favorite of hers since she was a kid and it also signifies that it's you that makes you magic – it's why you're here.

The book *Brandstarter*™ by Laura Wallace has helped Sarah to put her head in the game and take her business to the next level. The workbook helped her to come up with a logo when she didn't know what to do. She credits it with giving her the ability to think of things she hadn't thought of before.

HEALTH AND WELLNESS

"Health and Fitness is a life-long journey."

JULIE HARRIS

BEYOND THE MIC

Episode #50 – Julie Harris – Jules Fit Club

What You Can Get Out of Working with a Personal Trainer

Julie Harris

With a dad who was an opera singer, Julie Harris (https://www.pinterest.com/julesfitclub/) had the unique opportunity to grow up all over the country. When she got her degree in Exercise Science, she took a job with a fitness corporation, which gave her additional opportunities to travel. She eventually transferred to a job in Utah with a wellness company. While she loved her job, she just didn't feel settled in with where she wanted to go. It was when she moved to Colorado to work with a health plan that she met her husband and ended up moving to Frederick, Maryland where he grew up.

Julie got into running at a young age but struggled with liking her body. Unfortunately, this spiraled into problems with anorexia and bulimia over the years. Even when she became a personal trainer, she still struggled with her eating disorders. Jules Fit Club was born when she decided that it was time to share how she faced her struggles, so she could help others overcome any similar issues they might be having.

What You Can Get Out of Working with a Personal Trainer

Although there are lots of great trainers and programs out there to help people with fitness, Julie felt that there was a disconnect among them between the mind and body. It's important for people to understand that the mind controls the body. When we have negative thoughts, that's what impacts our health and fitness. It's always been her goal to bring this new approach to the fitness industry.

Julie starts off with getting to know her clients and understanding their barriers. By knowing their personal background, she can understand where they're coming from to create a personal program that is customized to them.

Part of her work involves identifying small steps that her clients can take to match their lifestyle and achieve success. She encourages constant communication with her clients, and she lets people train on their own at home or in the gym of their choice. They are still held accountable to her, and she helps them make adjustments and changes along the way to make sure the program fits with what they're trying to accomplish.

Julie's philosophy is that exercise is medicine and fitness is healing. She is currently working towards her dietician credentials so that she can incorporate nutrition into her programs. She wants her clients to see her programs as flexible and not as a hindrance. It's not something that they should feel they have to do, but something they can fit successfully into their life.

The Mind & Body Connection

Julie was first introduced to the concept of the mind and body connection by reading the book, *Quantum Healing* by Deepak Chopra. It helped her to learn about how the mind and body can connect and how that can help to create calm in a chaotic world.

"People aren't who they are because of where they are. People are where they are because of who they are."

FRANCINE SHAW

HEALTH AND WELLNESS

Episode #54 – Francine Shaw – Food Safety Training Solutions

A Field Trip to Help Improve Food Safety

Francine Shaw

Francine Shaw (https://foodsafetytrainingsolutions.net/) has had connections to the food service industry her entire life. Her grandparents had a convenience store where people would come to get their essentials, pump gas, and hang out on the front porch to chat with their neighbors. Her parents also owned a grocery store.

Francine's first job was also in the food service industry, and she was so successful there that she was able to work herself up to executive management. She left that job with the intention of getting out of the industry altogether but found that she missed it and the interaction it gave her with others. As a result, she started Food Safety Training Solutions in 2008.

A Field Trip to Help Improve Food Safety

A big part of Francine's work is in educating people on the importance of food safety for both individuals and businesses. She states that the perfect opportunity for her training would be for her to take a group of people as well as business owners on an educational field trip.

She would start the group off at a personal residence, and they would go into the kitchen. She would explain what they should and shouldn't have there and then move to the refrigerator and then to the cabinets. She would review expiration dates as well as explain the differences between "use by," "sell by," and "best by" dates that often confuse us at the grocery stores. She would also look for any dish towels or sponges and explain why they can be either good or bad.

Next, she would take the group to a convenience store, grocery store, a restaurant, or anyplace that serves food. Naturally, she would go into the kitchen and discuss what business owners should be looking for. She would also demonstrate proper hand washing and look at temperatures at which food was stored and cooked.

For the final part of the field trip, Francine would want to introduce everyone to people in a specific focus group. The group would be comprised of individuals who have lost a parent, a child, or another friend or family member due to food-borne illness. It would serve as a reminder of the consequences of what can happen when we don't pay attention to food safety guidelines.

Francine primarily works with organizations, but she also works with individual groups like a local PTA or a church who frequently hold potlucks. They will work with them to ensure that their events are safe and reduce any potential for health issues related to food preparation.

For some organizations, Francine's company can help them to get a better rating on a health and safety inspection. But, in general, they work to ensure that they a running a better establishment for both their safety and for the safety of the public.

HEALTH AND WELLNESS

"I Live in Hope"

CHRISTINA MURPHY

Episode #56 – Christina Murphy – Can Do With Lyme, LLC

What Everyone Should Know About Lyme Disease

Christina Murphy

Christina Murphy (http://www.candowithlyme.com/) stems from Washington D.C. where her parents were language translators for different governmental bodies. She was sent to boarding school, and she developed a love for horses, history, gardening, and herbs. She was once the head gardener at Schifferstadt Architectural Museum and was also on the board for the Frederick County Landmarks Foundation.

From 2007 – 2009, Christina's health started to change. She was having trouble seeing, talking, and walking, and her symptoms became unbearable. All the doctors she was seeing gave her remedies that only acted as a band-aid and she ended up getting worse. In 2009, her husband changed jobs, and they had to change health insurance plans. She was forced to go to a new doctor due to the change, but it worked in her favor. They tested her for Lyme disease when no one else had before. With the diagnosis, she was able to put a name on what was wrong and start to get the help she needed to feel better.

What Everyone Should Know About Lyme Disease

After Christina's diagnosis, she knew that she didn't want anyone to go through what she had. As a result of her illness, she lost her job at the museum, lost her place on the board of the foundation, and she wasn't able to take care of her family like she used to. Her desire to help and educate people on Lyme disease led to her certification as a Wellness Coach, which also led to her starting her business, Can Do With Lyme, LLC.

HEALTH AND WELLNESS

Most people think that Lyme disease comes from being bitten by a tick, but it extends beyond that. You can actually get Lyme disease from being bitten by anything that has the bacteria. This could be a tick, a mite, a mosquito, a spider, and in some cases, lizards. The disease transfers from the saliva of the creature that carries the disease.

Although most of Christina's counterparts focus more on being a personal coach, she focuses more on educating her clients. For those that want to help prevent the contraction of Lyme disease, she recommends spraying your clothing with permethrin and letting them dry prior to going outdoors. If you're going camping, she also recommends spraying it on your tent as well. You can find it at a lumber store or your local discount store. Or, if you prefer not to use chemicals or insecticides, you can also use a blend of lemongrass and eucalyptus to spray on clothing instead.

Christina also states that not everyone gets the "bullseye" rash that is commonly touted as a sign of the disease. In fact, only 9% of people who have Lyme disease get the rash. In addition to the rash, you should also look for symptoms like headaches, high fever, and flu.

If you do get tested, keep in mind that the tests being used to detect Lyme aren't really designed for it. They can give a false-positive, so you should have a second test done if that's the case for you.

Christina also recommends a change in your diet if you contract the disease. You should eat gluten-free, sugar-free, and dairy-free, as those elements will actually feed the bacteria. Once you stop feeding it, the bacteria will die off.

For every ten people who get diagnosed with Lyme disease, another nine have it but aren't documented. This is an unfortunate statistic as the earlier the disease is detected, the better it can be treated. Christina even states that if you can catch the bug that bit you, it may be helpful to test it to see if it has the disease. Part of the services her business provides is the ability to test the bug for the disease as well as providing information on where to go to find a good doctor.

Living in Hope

Christina's favorite quote is one of her own and it's one she lives by, "I live in hope." It's something that reminds her of the fact that every day there's one glimmer of hope. She's also incorporated this belief into her book, *Embracing Healing*.

HEALTH AND WELLNESS

"Can you remember who you were before the world told you who you should be?" Danielle LaPorte

---

RAE ROACH

BEYOND THE MIC

Episode #58 – Rae Roach – Women Helping Women Retreats

Finding Your True, Authentic Self

Rae Roach

Although Rae Roach (https://www.facebook.com/womenhelpingwomenretreats/) has lived in nine states, she considers Oklahoma to be her home. Her grandparents had a farm there and its where she spent every summer and holidays with them. She had several careers early in life as she traveled on her journey of trying to find herself.

Rae eventually went back to school to study law and worked in the field. An attorney she was working with was appointed as the General Counsel for the Securities and Exchange Commission. He asked her to go to Washington D.C. with him to become his personal assistant, so she accepted and made the move. After his appointment was over, he moved to Wall Street, so she moved to Manhattan to continue her role as his assistant. With this last move, family tragedies took place that changed her life permanently, which is what led her to start Women Helping Women Retreats.

Finding Your True, Authentic Self

During Rae's journey to finding herself, she met the founder of Empowered Women International. They were having a pitch competition where people could pitch their business and have the opportunity to win an entrepreneurial training for success class. Rae was already talking with a friend about doing a one-day retreat to help women, so she entered the contest and won.

The 6-month training class was a godsend for Rae, and it helped her to find the core of who she was. She realized that she was led by intellect all her life, and not by her heart.

Rae states that no matter where you are or what you're doing, women do too much. They constantly give to others before they give to themselves. It causes them to live life based on other's expectations or by what others think their life should be.

Rae holds her retreats nestled in nature so that all the busy, hustle-bustle aspects of life are left behind for attendees to focus on themselves without distractions. The experience is designed to connect women to their mind, body, spirit, and purpose through energizing and educational programs. It's done in a soothing, supportive way in order to for women to rediscover their natural feminine energy and strength.

This supportive environment is emphasized by a group of like-minded attendees who guide each other through ways to heal and achieve inner peace so that they can find their true, authentic self.

Overall, the retreat is a gift of self-awareness and personal development that can carry you throughout your everyday life. Through the event, attendees can learn and practice a method to achieve peace and clarity and use it in their daily lives as they go forward. As a result, a community of women is created to bring them into a safe, peaceful, and comfortable space that allows them to heal and reconnect their mind, body, and soul.

Embracing Personal Freedom

Rae cites the book *The Four Agreements* by Don Miguel Ruiz as one she's read several times. The book uncovers the source of self-limiting beliefs so that they can be resolved. It then goes into how people can transform their lives and embrace personal freedom, happiness, and love.

"Everything we do is Energy."

JOYCE RENNER

HEALTH AND WELLNESS

Episode #60 – Joyce Renner – Body and Sole Wellness

Understanding Reiki and Reflexology for Healing

Joyce Renner

Joyce Renner (http://www.bodyandsolewellness.com/) has lived in Middletown, Maryland her whole life. She volunteers at the local fire department and loves to read and continue her education.

A few years ago, some friends introduced her to reflexology. They loved it and encouraged her to give it a try. When she had her first session, Joyce thought it was an amazing, relaxing, and calming experience. After a few more sessions, she tried to find a place that taught reflexology but was unsuccessful.

Instead, she decided to investigate other holistic modalities like reiki and acupuncture. In July 2010, she was able to find a Reiki master nearby and took a level one reiki class over a weekend. She focused on that for a few years and eventually found a school that taught reflexology near Baltimore. She took basic classes then moved up to advanced studies, which led to her achieving national certification in 2015.

Understanding Reiki and Reflexology for Healing

Reiki is the process of balancing the body through chakras, which are energy fields in the body. While reflexology is the process of thumb and finger techniques to apply pressure to flex points on the feet and hands that correspond with areas on the body. For instance, the big toe connects to your head, which includes your sinuses and neck. Through the feet and hands, she can connect to all areas of the body such as the heart, lungs, intestines, spine, and hips as well as systems like the endocrine and nervous systems.

These practices are so connected to the body that a Reiki master can sense trouble areas within the body. They will scan the body with their hands and can feel its energy. A trouble area will often radiate heat allowing the Reiki master to pinpoint where work needs to be done. Some might consider the process to be almost like a combination of chiropractic and massage therapy.

Everything we do is energy, and it can get off-balance in our everyday lives. We put too much stress on our bodies by not eating right or not sleeping enough. The stress and worry we experience creates an unhealthy environment for our body that ultimately leads to illness and disease.

The practice of reflexology can increase oxygen and circulation while also inducing relaxation. It is about relaxing, repairing the body, relieving pain, and maintaining homeostasis. By putting the body's natural energy back into balance, a client can experience firsthand how these ancient practices can benefit them and improve overall health.

As Joyce points out, it's very important to pay attention to what our bodies are telling us. She often has to remind people of this, so they can fully appreciate how her work is helping them to heal.

Healing Your Life

Joyce references the book, *You Can Heal Your Life* by Louise Hay, as a source of inspiration. The concept of the book fits perfectly with her business and the power we all have within us to heal.

HEALTH AND WELLNESS

"The notion of failure is always fiction." From *Travels in a Stone Canoe* with Harvey Arden and Steve Wall

DIANA KAYE

BEYOND THE MIC

Episode #62 – Diana Kaye – Terressentials

Why Organic Products are a Better Option for Our Overall Health

Diana Kaye

For over 26 years, Diana Kaye (http://www.terressentials.com/) has focused on educating the public about dangerous chemicals in our environment through her business Terressentials. After being diagnosed with cancer at the young age of 29, she realized she loved life too much to die. This led her down a path filled with research and discoveries that would not only help her to heal, but to create her own certified organic personal care products business.

She attributes her partner with helping her throughout her diagnosis and treatment. He helped her with the research and uncovering how she could recover from radical chemotherapy treatments. Now, they own the business together, and it's their life-long mission to provide healthy, safe, and genuine organic products to their customers.

Why Organic Products are a Better Option for Our Overall Health

Any of us knows that we can walk into any drug store or big discount store to buy personal products such as shampoo, skin care, lotions, and deodorants. So, what's the difference between those products and the ones that Diana produces and offers through Terressentials?

According to Diana, there are more differences between the two than most people realize. The truth is that the majority of products on the market contain chemical ingredients that are derived from gasoline by-products. Out of a 55-gallon barrel of crude oil, only 2.5 gallons of gasoline is created. The remainder of that original barrel is transformed via energy-intensive ~~pollutive~~ and polluting industrial processes into a variety of chemicals, including plastics such as polyester, acrylic, nylon, acetate and vinyls for clothing and for use in foamy shampoos, hair conditioners and styling products and hair dyes and bleaches, in body lotions, sunscreens, makeup, and the cleaning products we use throughout our home.

Up to 60% of the chemicals found in these products are absorbed into our skin when we come into contact with them. In the instances when we use these products when our skin is wet, like for shampoo, even more of these products are absorbed into our bodies and our bloodstream. And in some cases, the chemicals in our cleaning and personal care products are called volatile compounds and are gaseous. That means that just by having these products in our home, not only are we exposed to them, but we're inhaling them each and every day.

The toxic effects of daily exposure to these conventional chemicals isn't only to us individually as humans. When we use conventional chemical products, the chemicals are absorbed into our bodies and can be released into the air whereupon we inhale them and they are moved into our bloodstream. The chemicals are also washed down the drain and into our waterways, which is seriously affecting we humans and the wildlife and marine life that live in or drink from all of our lakes, rivers, streams, bays and oceans.

The products that Diana and her partner create are all handcrafted in small batches. She likens her business to a small organic bakery crafting authentic certified organic personal care products. She uses truly natural elements such as clays, salts and minerals, along with certified organic oils, botanical butters, beeswax, herbal extracts and essential oils that work synergistically to clean, soothe, and nourish the skin without the harmful effects of man-made chemicals or industrial processing waste by-products.

Respecting the Land & Protecting the Future

Diana recommends the book *Travels in a Stone Canoe* by Harvey Arden and Steve Wall and cites it as one that reflects the values that she holds true. The book is about two journalists who venture out to interview Native American elders or "wisdom keepers" as they are known in their society. The only problem was that the elders didn't want to talk to them, so the journalists had to earn their trust before they would share their stories with them.

A quote from the book also stands out for Diana. "The notion of failure is always a fiction, a false self-judgment, and that on the path of the wisdom keeper, there's only the closing of one's possibility and the opening of infinite others."

That quote is actually labeled in the book as "The Original Instructions for Being Human." For Diana, it reflects her beliefs about sustainability, protecting the earth and respecting the land. "It's our job not to pollute the earth as we need to leave it for our children who are our future."

HEALTH AND WELLNESS

"We drink for a well not of our own creation."

DANNY FARRAR

BEYOND THE MIC

Episode #63 – Danny Farrar – Soldierfit

There's More to Fitness Than Being Fit

Danny Farrar

Danny Farrar (https://soldierfit.com/) comes from a difficult upbringing, but it's what has shaped him into the successful businessman he is today. He went into the army and was only five minutes away from the Pentagon on 9/11 when the plane hit. He was part of the team that was charged with removing remains from the building, and that stayed with him. After he got out of the army, he struggled to find work and ended up homeless.

Partly for wanting revenge for 9/11 and the fact that he missed military life, Danny enlisted to be a Reserve. He went overseas to Iraq from 2005 – 2006 and returned home to join the local fire department. At the same time, he also started DDT Fitness with his friends. The business grew and evolved from Danny's desire to provide cross-fit training to people at an affordable rate. Soldierfit was born, and now they offer classes at about a third of the price of their competition.

There's More to Fitness Than Being Fit

Earlier in this book, we featured Cary Lederer (Chapter #46) who is Vice President of Operations for Soldierfit, and if you remember she emphasized how the company's vision statement states nothing about fitness. As CEO and Founder, it's how Danny has structured the company and it's the same philosophy that's still important to him today.

As Danny says, everyone knows the importance of being fit. The more physically fit you are, the better you're able to perform. But for him, fitness is also about being a stronger community. When you're in a community of strong, fit people, you know you can rely on them, and they've got your back.

HEALTH AND WELLNESS

Although a workout will improve how you look on the outside, if you're not focused on something more than a superficial goal, you won't grow as a person. It's never been about who looks the best because that's not what makes you happy. For Danny, being fit is more about being a positive influence on your community. It's this mindset that he attributes to the fact that over 98% of his employees were once members. They've bought into the culture and believed in it enough to want to become a part of it.

Giving Back and Doing the Right Thing

Danny cites the book *Rich Dad, Poor Dad* by Robert Kiyosaki as a major influence when he was starting his business. It taught him that having to be present all the time followed the characteristics of a job, not a business. This thought inspired him to go from one-on-one clients to doing group classes to free up more of his time.

The quote Danny refers to often is, "We drink from a well not of our own creation." He strongly feels that if a person was left alone to their own devices, that they would do the right thing. In today's society, it can be easy to be cynical and think of the world as a bad, dark place. He believes that this isn't true and that the average person wants to and will do the right thing.

"Be the change that you wish to see in the world."
Gandhi

DR. ALISON BOMBA

HEALTH AND WELLNESS

Episode #68 – Dr. Alison Bomba – Psychologist

Taking Care of Our Mental Health

Dr. Alison Bomba

Although she grew up near Erie, Pennsylvania, Dr. Alison Bomba (https://www.drbomba.com/) has been living in Frederick, Maryland since 2001. She knew from a young age that she wanted to become a child psychologist, especially from babysitting and enjoying working with children.

Prior to becoming a licensed psychologist, Dr. Bomba obtained a lot of varying employment experiences. These roles included home-based therapy for autistic children, working at a therapeutic pre-school, crisis work, and neuropsychological testing. After getting her doctorate, she joined a group practice and worked there for nine years. In October 2015, she opened up her private practice where she works with children as young as 3 years old, teenagers, and young adults.

Taking Care of Our Mental Health

As Dr. Bomba emphasizes, taking care of our mental health is just as important as taking care of our physical health. Part of doing this involves eliminating the stigma around seeking mental healthcare. We all need a little extra help sometimes, and that's okay. Any traumatic, stressful events in our lives have the potential to lead to difficulties and can negatively impact career performance, sleep, physical health, mood, and overall functioning.

Another thing to keep in mind is that the confidential nature of psychotherapy sessions provides a safe, therapeutic environment in which to process difficult material. A common misconception is that a psychologist gives advice. In fact, their role is to listen with a non-biased, non-judgmental ear to help raise insight and perspectives to assist people with coming up with their own perspectives. This will help them to make their own decisions to improve their lives.

We've all seen, especially in recent years, how things can happen in our world that we can't control or change. But we can learn how to control how we think of those events and the way we respond to them. Dr. Bomba says that it's important for us to learn to go on when we experience failure or when bad things happen. We must learn to tolerate the discomfort of stress, anxiety, or disappointment rather than escape difficult situations. The tolerance we build will lead to resilience.

In Dr. Bomba's practice, she uses Cognitive Behavioral Therapy (CBT), which is a very effective evidence-based treatment. It's also the recommended therapy for anxiety and depression among other presenting problems. The treatment helps people learn to re-train their brains to think more adaptively and to modify their behaviors and overall functioning. Homework is often prescribed in between sessions, and it arms people with skills they can use for the rest of their lives.

The Only Thing We Can Control is Ourselves

Dr. Bomba says that the quote from Gandhi, "Be the change that you wish to see in the world," is inspiring for her. For her, it places emphasis on ownership, empowerment, and taking action. At the end of the day when things aren't going the way we want them to, the only thing we can control is ourselves. We might as well serve as good role models for others while effecting positive change where we can.

HEALTH AND WELLNESS

"Live a life worth telling a Story about." Todd Durkin

DR. JOSH FUNK

BEYOND THE MIC

Episode #71 – Dr. Josh Funk – Rehab 2 Reform

Empowering People to Be in Control of How They Feel

Dr. Josh Funk

Having played nine team sports growing up, Dr. Josh Funk (http://rehab2perform.com/) was on the path to living a life in the sports community. When he went to Ohio State where he played lacrosse. It was his experience there that helped him discover his passion for health and fitness.

In his sophomore year, he suffered a shoulder injury during practice that changed his perspective on the career he pursued. After x-rays and an MRI, he was told that he had a small rotator cuff tear and a torn labrum. He could continue playing, but he would need surgery at the end of the season. He decided to get a second opinion and saw a doctor that told Dr. Josh that he had seen worse injuries do well with physical therapy. He went for that option and worked on his shoulder all summer and hasn't had a problem with it since.

Empowering People to Be in Control of How They Feel

Dr. Josh's experience with physical therapy led him to pursue his clinical doctorate at the University of Maryland. After graduating, he worked at private practice clinics that helped him understand what it was like to work with people. By seeing what worked with them, he also learned what he liked and didn't like about the work he was doing.

From his work at those clinics, he came up with the idea to do something that he didn't see a lot of, which was a hybrid-style health and wellness clinic. He started Rehab 2 Perform in 2014 where half of the facility looks like a gym with workout equipment, and the other half has treatment tables and various recovery modalities.

One thing he learned by working in physical therapy was that the main risk for injury is a previous injury. This fact made him realize that the average clinic wasn't doing as good of a job as they could with taking people to a high-level of function. With Rehab 2 Perform, they help their clients deal with pain and dysfunction. They are then moved to the other side of the facility to make sure clients are able to do the things they want to do once they leave treatment.

For Dr. Josh, it's much more than looking at a specific injury. If all he focused on were an injured shoulder or knee, he would be overlooking something. Our bodies have a lot of ways to compensate and work around pain in order to allow us to function. It's why he does a full head-to-toe evaluation and assessment to get a big picture of what that person can and can't do and how to relieve pain. Overall, he provides education and empowers people so that they can be in control of any limitations, how they feel, and how they perform.

Dr. Josh takes this role seriously and wants to create people who are more efficient and find it easy to do the things they do on a daily basis so that they can enjoy life more. An injury can also affect us on a psychological and social level, and it's his job to get his clients back to their normal everyday lives.

Expanding Boundaries & Making an Impact

The quote by Todd Durkin, "Live a life worth telling a story about," is one that has changed Dr. Josh's perspective. It's how he approaches his free time, especially by saying "yes" to everything, and "no" a lot less often. This idea has allowed him to expand his boundaries and enjoy more of what he likes to do.

When he gets older, and into retirement age, Dr. Josh wants to be able to look back and feel that he's left an impact. He wants to guide the next generation of people as well as change the trajectory of the people he's interacted with throughout his career.

BEYOND THE MIC

ENTREPRENEURSHIP

An Entrepreneur tends to bite off more than he can chew hoping he'll quickly learn how to chew it. – Roy Ash

Introduction – Entrepreneurship

This is probably my favorite section because we have such a WIDE variety of people in various industries that we interviewed under the 'Entrepreneur' label.

Although everyone featured in *Beyond the Mic* is a true Entrepreneur, those in the other sections have a framework more like a traditional business. The guests featured in this section definitely act outside of the traditional business model when running their company.

The beautiful thing and what I found true when interviewing all these guests is their passion for what they do and how they help others. Entrepreneurs don't work 9 am to 5 pm. Entrepreneurs are *always* working. When they aren't running the day-to-day operations of their business, then they are executing on strategies that can help with long-term growth in their business.

Entrepreneurs are cut from a different mold. They are innovators. They are risk takers. They are visionaries.

I am so very thrilled to introduce to you those Entrepreneurs in this section of *Beyond the Mic*. Get ready because you are about to meet some incredible individuals!

Cheers.

ENTREPRENEURSHIP

"Podcasts help you create relationships with people you normally wouldn't meet."

RYAN SLOPER

BEYOND THE MIC

Episode #1 – Ryan Sloper – Media Personality/Duck Donuts

Ryan Sloper

Ryan Sloper (Email: ryantsloper@gmail.com) is a radio personality, and veteran podcaster of the show Real Estate 360 Live on iTunes. Ryan was originally driving for an hour to an hour and a half for his weekly show on terrestrial radio. He was tired of losing a whole day out of the week to make the trek, and that's when he realized something had to change. At the time, podcasting was just starting to gain traction and reach audiences. He had the choice of doing his radio show from home by building a $15,000 studio in his house to avoid commuting to the radio station or do a podcast for significantly less. Podcasting became his obvious choice, and now he has the ability to reach his audience 24/7.

The Evolution and Benefits of Podcasts

Since Ryan was the one who got me into listening to podcasts, it was only natural that I invite to be the guest on my first podcast episode. What he showed me is that by having a podcast, you can reach your audience on their computer or mobile device anytime. At first, podcasting was geared towards marketers and entrepreneurs, but now you can find a podcast on iTunes or Stitcher on just about any topic.

Ryan and I listen to similar podcasts as we use them mostly as a way to learn more about others doing what we do. Some of the podcasts we both love include Entrepreneur on Fire by John Lee Dumas, The Tim Ferriss Show, and The James Altucher Show. We both agree that listening to podcasts is that you discover more about the interviewer as well as the interviewee that you likely wouldn't have heard anywhere else. You get a unique insight into how their started or grew their business, what drives them, strategies they use, and their core values. In fact, it helps me to know that I'm not alone in having days where I struggle or that something didn't work out quite as planned.

Due to the wide variety of topics now covered on podcasts, you can literally tap into whatever's interesting to you at any given time. And what makes them so convenient is that you don't have to wait until you have time to read about a subject. You can listen to a podcast on your phone, computer, or in the car. Ryan also mentioned to me that it helps him discover like-minded people and it's that connection that keeps him tuning in for future episodes.

The Importance of Creating an Experience for Your Audience

It surprised me when Ryan announced that he was going in a completely different direction for a new venture. Even though Ryan is known for his work in the real estate community, he told me that he is opening a donut shop!

Why would a real estate guy open a donut shop? Well, it really happened for two reasons. One was the need for a breakfast place in his local community. The other is about something he experienced on a recent family vacation.

Given his location in Northern Virginia, it's common for people in that area to vacation in the Outer Banks. While there, he saw family members buying Duck Donuts by the box day after day. He soon realized he needed to see what was so special about them that made his family spend hundreds of dollars on donuts over the course of their vacation. By going to the shop, he could instantly see the appeal. Kids were lurking at the window to see how the donuts were made. Customers were waiting in line for 45 minutes or more to place their order. It wasn't just that the donuts were fresh and made to order, they were creating an experience for their customers.

Ryan realized that he could bring not just any breakfast place to his community, but one that people would flock to because of the experience. What really sealed the deal was that since most people frequented the Outer Banks, the branding was already in place since they knew what to expect when they saw a Duck Donut shop.

I compared this to a recent trip of mine to Disney World. The staff went out of their way to make sure my family and I enjoyed the time we spent there. Nowhere was this more true when my son wanted two stuffed animals, but only had money for one. An employee overheard our conversation and offered to let "Mickey Mouse" help pay for the second toy.

Why is experience so important to your audience and your customers? It's because it's what keeps your customers coming back to you and not your competition. Recently, I was showing a house that had been vacant. Upon arriving, I heard water running. Definitely not a good sign. I located the source, which unfortunately was a flooded basement. After getting the water pumped out, fixing the plumbing, and having drywall replaced and painted in a very short time, the seller was beyond happy with how my team and I stepped up to make sure that the house was shown as scheduled.

It's these types of experiences that help people decide if it's a person or a business they want to work with. And when those stories of how they were treated are shared, it can lead to more business and relationships that wouldn't have happened otherwise. It's interestingly the same with podcasts. Listening to them helps you to develop an affinity with other like-minded individuals you wouldn't normally have access to. It's about starting with your story and creating a relationship that differentiates you from your competition. When people see you want to help them, it keeps them coming back for more.

"To be successful, you have to exhaust all resources to achieve that success."

ANNIE MAIN

BEYOND THE MIC

Episode #2 – Annie Main – A. Marie Imagery

Annie Main

Annie Main (Email: annie@amarieimagery.com URL: amarieimagery.com) is a photographer who specializes in real estate photography. When she was younger, she ventured into photography, but when her camera broke in a few short weeks, that dream was shelved for a number of years. It wasn't until she was married that she decided it was time to give it a try again. After a few unsuccessful attempts of trying to capture people, she ventured into real estate where she was able to use the camera to serve her. Although a challenge at times, Annie enjoys telling a visual story of the property she shoots with photos.

Using Staging to Create Trust with Your Customers

I've been working with Annie for about eight years, and she's my go-to person to snap pictures of the properties I show. During our conversation, we discussed how the work she does can differ greatly depending on whether a house has been staged or not.

As a real estate photography, Annie knows that it's her job to show the property in the best possible light. That's where a staging company can come in and make her job much easier. But when there's not enough time or resources to use a staging company, her work becomes much more involved. It takes her more time to take and edit the photos. Without that professional touch, the pictures don't have the same quality. Also, the house won't look as clean as it should, and the rooms will often look smaller.

A homebuyer, as with most other purchases, will buy based on emotions. If a house looks too lived in, it might make them look elsewhere. As Annie takes photos, she tried to put herself in the buyer's shoes and will avoid anything that may detract them from buying. After taking the photos, she's tasked with the responsibility of choosing the best pictures that jump out and tell the story of the house. Of course, sometimes she needs to choose pictures based on information instead of visual appeal. This could be highlighting a uniquely-sized space within the home or to reflect the size of a basement.

One story comes to mind where I showed a house for a couple interested in buying where only the husband showed up. He had his wife on the phone and was telling her, "Yes, honey, the house looks just like the pictures." What was interesting is based on what he saw, and what she knew from the photos, I had a full price offer by the end of the night! I don't think the wife saw the home until inspection, which is unheard of in the real estate industry. It made me realize that when you have the right resources in place and you "stage" your business to reflect your best possible light, regardless of niche or industry, people will trust you sight unseen.

Tempering Your Expectations to Meet Those of Your Clients

As entrepreneurs, we often want to under-promise and over-deliver. While there's nothing wrong with that or with trying to make our customers happy, those expectations can derail us and make life much harder than it should be. It's also what Annie mentioned as one of the things that's been hardest as she builds her business.

Annie admitted that her expectations are often way higher than that of her clients. For instance, a client might want something done within a week, but she'll have everything ready within 1 – 2 days. Even if someone tells her not to rush, she has a difficult time taking that long to get something accomplished. It's at those moments where she has to take a deep breath and accept her client's word for it. I've found this to be a common theme among fellow entrepreneurs. I think it just follows along with the same type of mindset that guides us to go out and start a business in the first place.

It also matches with what Annie told me about a certain phrase she says often. As entrepreneurs, we juggle a lot, and it can be easy to complain or get frustrated when things don't go right. Annie's motto is that we really don't have a right to complain if we haven't exhausted all the resources to fix the problem. It's only when we do that we can rest easy at night knowing we've done everything possible to resolve whatever issue we're having.

Additional Facts About Annie

- Annie has the capability to track people who do virtual tours so her clients can view stats on how many people looked at the listing and the referral sites to help them streamline their marketing efforts.
- She also does real estate flyers for a handful of her clients, but her main focus is on photography.
- She's originally from Wisconsin, but she's also lived in Kansas, California, and Maryland. In fact, she spent some of her childhood in Maryland, and she now lives just a mile from where she grew up!

ENTREPRENEURSHIP

"You can do anything you set your mind to."

MIKE FITZGERALD

BEYOND THE MIC

Episode #9 – Mike Fitzgerald – Entrepreneur – Gideon Properties & Fitzgerald Funding

The True Essence of an Entrepreneur

Mike Fitzgerald

Mike Fitzgerald (URL: https://www.gideonprop.com/ or https://www.REIAUnited.com/) is just one of those people who has always been an entrepreneur. When he was 5, he wandered off. His mom found him at a nearby construction site asking questions and he was never afraid to ask strangers for candy. He comes from a large family that struggled to make ends meet, which is what led him to start a paper route at the age of 9. When he was told that he could make $2 for every new subscriber he brought in, he was on it! He was able to bring in over 1,000 subscribers and won at least a dozen contests for his efforts. They actually had to split his route in half twice because there were so many subscriptions to deliver to! From then on, he was always striving to make money, help his family, and help others.

The True Essence of Entrepreneur

For anyone who's met Mike, they can see that he embodies the true essence of an entrepreneur. He's energetic, vibrant, and never backs down from the opportunity to meet people or start a conversation. It's this attitude that he attributes to his success.

But the main thing that stands out with Mike, isn't his attitude. It's his love for helping others and nowhere is this more true than with the work he's done to help his community. As a real estate investor, Mike works with residential and commercial properties. A commercial property known as the Grand Piano Building in Hagerstown, MD, was in bad shape. When it was brought to his attention, it was an almost vacant property with only two tenants, and they were both ready to leave. The inspection report showed that there were 193 leaks from the roof down to the first floor!

Mike was able to go in and start making repairs to the property. As he refurbished the space, not only did he keep those 2 tenants from leaving, but he was also able to attract new tenants. The building quickly filled up to where only 2 spaces were left vacant. He considers it a boutique office building, where the tenants can also get a break on the rent through the city. He also works diligently to promote all of his tenants knowing that when their business thrives, the entire community benefits.

It's this attitude that moves away from a focus on money and towards building a stronger community. His work with this one building has brought life back into the city and he's stretched those efforts to other communities. Mike also has additional businesses where he coaches a small group of people who are interested in real estate investing. He also owns FitzgeraldFunding.com that lends money to those looking to start a new real estate business.

As entrepreneurs, of course we want to create a legacy for our children and provide for our families. Yet, it's just as important to promote what's in our surroundings and impact the future for the next generation.

"You can do anything you sent your mind to."

If you ask Mike, he would tell you that he never would have thought to be where he is today. As a kid, he often daydreamed and struggled to pay attention in class and he only had a 2.3 GPA in high school. So, where did his success come from?

He'll be the first to tell you that it's all about mindset. He envisioned what he wanted to do and how he could make a difference and went to work. It's his belief that anyone regardless of knowledge or background who has the right mindset, has a dream, and is willing to face any challenges and charge through them, they will do great.

"What you think about, you bring about."

CARESSA FLANNERY

Episode #16 – Caressa Flannery – Owner – Create A Pulse Marketing

Giving Back to the Community Through Entrepreneurship

Caressa Flannery

Caressa Flannery (URL: http://www.createapulsemarketing.com/ Email: createapulse@comcast.net) is well-known in her community. In fact, she's been called an "uber-volunteer" due to the massive amount of work she's done in Frederick, Maryland. Over the last few years, she's volunteered for the Downtown Frederick Partnership and the Alive @ 5 series. She was also on the board for Celebrate Frederick and acted as chair for Frederick's 4th of July for four years. Caressa has a degree in Family Studies, which she attributes to her ability to connect and interact with others. It's given her insight into people and how to build strong relationships with them to create a successful business.

A Full Set of Marketing Services to Serve the Community

Caressa has worked in a variety of sales and marketing positions over the years. In 2004, she decided to take a leap of faith into entrepreneurship and start her own business, Create A Pulse Marketing. And it's something that she wishes she had done much sooner. Her business offers an affordable marketing solution for the small businesses in town. Planning her high school reunion on Facebook gave her an unexpected connection to people online, and it has helped her to add on additional services to assist her clients.

One of the ways that Caressa is different from others providing similar services is that she's always willing to meet her clients in person whenever possible. Since she works from home, she doesn't have to worry about expensive office space. It's what also makes her services so affordable since she's able to pass those savings on to her clients.

Overall, what makes Caressa's business successful is her people-friendly approach to building relationships. Her list of long-term clients is proof that people like to work with her and how her connections have helped her grow her business. She's also been nicknamed "The Great Connector of Frederick" because she knows someone in just about every arena and can connect people regardless of their needs.

Caressa's exposure goes well beyond her social media presence. People see her everywhere given her dedication to volunteer efforts. She loves how her work supports non-profits to promote their cause and how that, in turn, benefits the community.

"What You Think About, You Bring About."

Caressa mentioned to me that she is constantly thinking towards the positive. She believes that the more positive your thoughts are, the more it will manifest in your life.

She also stated that the book, *Shut Up, Stop Whining, and Get a Life* by Larry Winget, has resonated with her. The book came out around the same time that she launched her business, so it was a very timely resource for her to have access to. One thing that stood out for her is that in the book, Larry Winget mentions that the key components to success in your business and personal life are love and your service to others. That point mirrors the fact that she's always been altruistic and focused on giving back to the community.

"Just like riding a bike, once you learn, you never forget."

MONICA MACCRACKEN

BEYOND THE MIC

Episode #18 – Monica MacCracken – Owner – Monica's Floral Designs

Money-Saving Flower Tips for the Consumer

Monica MacCracken

Monica MacCracken (URL: https://www.facebook.com/Monicas-Floral-Designs-119570438105967/) had the benefit of being introduced to the floral industry at a young age. At 14, her mom wanted her to gain experience by having a job, so she brought Monica to a florist nearby who was also a friend. Initially, she helped with sweeping floors, putting flowers away, pricing items, and keeping the shop clean. She continued working at the florist through high school and the more she was there, the more she was interested in floral design. She moved up to helping with cutting stems and putting away the flowers. She eventually learned how to prepare arrangements for sale. The shop did a lot of weddings, which helped her learn how to create bouquets and bridal arrangements for when she started her own business.

Money-Saving Flower Tips

One of the biggest challenges Monica faces with her business is ordering flowers that arrive fresh, look good, and are the right colors. Given that she often has to match a bride's color scheme, it's important that the flowers she's chosen match the expected vision.

Monica has offered some helpful tips that can help you have long-lasting flowers and save money:

- If you like tulips, then you also know that they tend to open quickly when placed in water. One way to avoid this is to put a penny in the water. It will prevent them from opening so they will last longer.

- For hydrangeas, they have a tendency to wilt quickly. To remedy this, cut the stem a little and completely submerge them upside down in a bucket of warm water for a few hours, and they will be restored.
- If you're working on a budget for a special event or wedding, try to keep within three types of flowers. This will give you depth and texture but also a way for your florist to assist you with a professional looking piece while making costs more affordable.

Monica is always willing to help her customers, especially when they're on a tight budget. She especially likes when someone is referred to her that has a vision but isn't sure of how to create it, she is able to provide them with a displays or bouquets that they can be happy with.

"Just Like Riding a Bike…."

Monica lives by the quote, "Just like riding a bike, once you learn, you never forget." It's one that is easy to apply both in life and in business. No matter how many times you fall, you can get back up and keep going. The more you keep trying, and the more you keep working, the better you'll get at it.

"I don't expect you to do what's easy. I expect you to do what's hard." Barack Obama

---

ANGELA OSTROFF

ENTREPRENEURSHIP

Episode #21 – Angela Ostroff – Owner – Bearly Marketing

Why You Should Outsource Your Online Marketing

Angela Ostroff

Angela Ostroff (URL: http://bearlymarketing.com/) has an extensive background in sales and marketing. Her initial experience came from when she worked for a furniture company, where she did retail sales in addition to marketing and social media. After working 50 – 60-hour weeks for years, she decided that it was time to venture out on her own but wasn't sure of what to do next. Angela started freelancing in content marketing, but it wasn't quite what she expected. After a client requested her help with Pinterest, she realized how much she enjoyed assisting clients with social media. Her business picked up, which allowed her to start hiring staff and opening an office for Bearly Marketing after 3 months in business.

The Benefits of Outsourcing Your Online Marketing Efforts

As a small business owner herself, Angela completely understands how business owners want to handle everything themselves. It's a difficult decision to start handing over tasks to someone new, but it's also necessary for expanding and growing your business. If it weren't for her decision to hire help, she would have never been able to handle over 300 clients as she does now. It's also something she wishes she had done sooner! Whether you hire someone or an agency, make sure you have someone who can take social media off your plate so you can focus on more strategic tasks.

If you do decide to outsource, make sure that you don't make a decision solely based on price. While it's great to stay within your budget, it's also important to ensure that your social media is professional and matches your brand. All too often, Angela sees companies that have hired a social media agency because they were cheap. Unfortunately, the posts often come off spammy, which can damage your reputation. Instead, make sure that you hire an agency that will take that extra step to reflect your brand and personal voice in your posts.

Another thing to keep in mind when you outsource your social media is to make sure that the agency is available to respond to your requests. If you need to do something quickly, you don't want to have to wait days or possibly weeks to get a response. Angela is in the office seven days a week, and I can attest to the fact that she is very good about responding to messages, as well as with offering ideas and suggestions.

Gaining the Inspiration to Outsource

Why do so many small business owners and entrepreneurs avoid hiring help for their business? For some, it's the fear that no one else will know their business as well as they do, and they worry something could go wrong. For others, they may feel like it's impossible because they can't afford the extra cost.

Regardless of the reason for avoiding the expansion of staff, Angela experienced this with her business and it's something I also experienced with mine. Angela points to the book, *The E-Myth* by Michael Gerber, as the resource that led her to start hiring staff. It was when she hired a salesperson that she realized that she could grow her business, which made life much easier!

"This too shall pass." Eckhart Tolle

VINNY LaBARBERA

BEYOND THE MIC

Episode #30 – Vinny La Barbera – CEO - imFORZA

Why Your Business Needs an Internet Marketing Strategy

Vinny La Barbera

Coming from a long line of entrepreneurs, Vinny La Barbera (URL: https://www.imforza.com/) was next in his family to start his own venture. After getting his degree at USC, he was working towards his MBA and got a part-time job at a web design company that was looking for project managers. Once he started working there, he realized that the client websites they were creating weren't generating leads. He took it upon himself to do the research to figure out how to change things and get the clients better results.

Through his success and determination, he built up their internet marketing division with services ranging from PPC to SEO and everything in between. The division went from being only him to 11 people who serviced accounts for about 8,000 real estate agents.

Why Businesses Need an Internet Marketing Strategy

Vinny sees a lot of businesses who try to do internet marketing, but they fail to achieve actual results. Having an internet marketing strategy can make a difference with being able to communicate effectively online in order to effectively reach a target audience. When it's done correctly, it outperforms everything else. It also is trackable with tools like Google Analytics, so you can easily see your results and progress.

Internet marketing also creates a channel of freedom. It's an opportunity for people who know how to leverage it. You can communicate your values to people who don't know anything about you, your business, or your product or service. It makes for a fantastic way to get a message to promote what you're trying to accomplish.

ENTREPRENEURSHIP

If you decide to partner with an internet marketing strategy like Vinny's, they should work directly with you to create opportunities to enhance results and offer recommendations. For imFORZA, these services often lead to business consulting since so many businesses operate solely online.

Great Resource & Advice for Entrepreneurs

Vinny points to the book, *Zero to One* by Peter Thiel, as an excellent resource for entrepreneurs. It shows you how to better plan for your business and grow it. He even goes so far to say that it should be part of any entrepreneurial curriculum, and honestly, I agree.

"This too shall pass" is a quote from Eckhart Tolle that Vinny feels you can apply to any situation in all aspects of life and business. It's a reminder that the tough times will happen, but they won't last. And the same goes for the good times. They won't last either, but it's a reminder to be grateful. If you start your day with gratitude, it keeps you focused and motivated towards achieving what you want to do.

"Just get the work done." Joe Plicka

GABRIELLE PASTOREK

ENTREPRENEURSHIP

Episode #32 – Gabrielle Pastorek – Freelance Author & Editor

Discovering Your Mission Critical

Gabrielle Pastorek

Gabrielle Pastorek (http://www.gabriellepastorek.com/) grew up in a small town in Pennsylvania. She rode horses and spent a lot of time doing barn duties, which helped to pay for her horse riding lessons. I hadn't realized that Gabrielle and I had this in common as I grew up on a horse farm. She went to school at Ohio University to escape from a small town and change her surroundings. She ended up getting homesick and returned to Pennsylvania to get her Master's degree in Fiction Writing. Before starting her freelance business, Gabrielle worked at a number of odd jobs including working at a bookstore, tutoring, being a nanny, and testing chemicals in people's swimming pool water!

Discovering Your Mission Critical

Working in a creative field can present its own unique challenges. Gabrielle wasn't a stranger to them, especially when she had to struggle with the rumors that having a writing career was difficult. She was also told that she would only find success if she went into teaching. Being immersed in that mindset overwhelmed her, but she continued undeterred.

It was one of her college professors that told her she needed to have a "Mission Critical." He also told her that if it she wanted to write, she would have to show up for it, and then everything would fall into place. She kept believing that by finding her "Mission Critical" it would work for her and it changed her whole mindset. Until her professor told her that, she had taken some freelance gigs but had doubts that they would sustain her. His words gave her the permission to make writing her career, and it helped steer her towards her passion.

Gabrielle has been a freelance author and editor for over seven years now. Along the way, her "Mission Critical" has provided her with a career she loves, and it allows her to help others. She once had a client who had an amazing story filled with heartache and drama that was to be published as a memoir. Her client was struggling to get the words right on paper and felt that her grammar wasn't as perfect as it should be. Gabrielle was able to help her frame the story and the words so that the story would be told to its fullest. Not only would this help the story to reach people, but it would also help others overcome their own challenges.

"Just Get the Work Done."

As a writer, it can be very easy to let your own voice keep you from writing and procrastinate the task entirely. A former professor offered Gabrielle encouragement and told her that even if she didn't feel like doing it, or if she didn't feel like she was good enough, just sit down, and get the work done. I think this mindset is critical for any entrepreneur who is not sure of their abilities or who are experiencing any doubts.

Gabrielle also credits the book, *Childhood in Other Neighborhoods* by Stuart Dybek. It's a collection of short stories by one of her favorite authors. When she sat down to read it for the first time, she instantly knew that writing was what she wanted to do.

"You have to constantly learn and have that motivation to continue to learn. Otherwise, you get stagnant."

KIM DOW

BEYOND THE MIC

Episode #36 – Kim Dow – Kalico Designs & Sass Magazine

Why You Should Invest in Marketing & Branding for Your Business

Kim Dow

Kim Dow (http://kalicodesign.com/ & http://www.sassmagazine.com/) is originally from Frederick, Maryland, and was destined for her current career path. She majored in Art with a focus in Graphic Design and previously worked at a graphic design studio in town. When she realized that there wasn't anywhere for her to grow there, she started her own studio, Kalico Designs, and hit the ground running! In spite of not taking any business courses, she was ready to go with her laptop and was able to grow her business from referrals.

Kim credits her success to her ability to learn by doing in addition to a lot of support from other business owners and entrepreneurs in the community. They were willing to mentor her through periods of trial and error, which made all the difference. After successfully running that business for about seven years, she branched out to start Sass Magazine. They highlight amazing women in the community, and the response has been overwhelmingly positive. With two businesses to run, Kim rarely has spare time, but she loves to dance, read, and travel.

Why You Should Invest in Marketing & Branding for Your Business

Kim states that too many businesses make the mistake of thinking of marketing and branding as an expense. Instead, she says that they should be looked at as an investment. If you're not willing to invest time and effort into your marketing, how can you expect your clients to invest in your business?

Another mistake business owners make is in trying to do the marketing and branding themselves. Overall, it's better to hire a professional. They have the expertise to get your site to stand out and speak for your business. As a business owner, your focus should be on running and growing your business. When you outsource this task, you can also utilize someone who has an outside perspective. Their work will create a presence for your business that will last for a long time, which is something that you likely won't get if you do it yourself.

A professional graphic designer or another professional who knows web design can create a strategy behind their work and build the visual side of it. It's more important for you to stick with what you know, as it's virtually impossible to be an expert at everything. Your focus is better utilized on your business and your vision for it.

Applying a Single Thought from Every Resource

Even though Kim is currently reading Drive by Daniel Pink, she told me that she's constantly reading and really doesn't have one book or quote that stands out to her. Instead, she says that it's more important for her to take something from every resource she employs.

Whether it's a quick article she reads online, a fiction novel, or a business-related book, she works towards figuring out a way to apply what she's learned from every resource.

"You have to take your opportunity when it's given to you to give back. And, be a leader."

JAY MASON

ENTREPRENEURSHIP

Episode #39 – Jay Mason – Realtor & Community Leader

How Entrepreneurship Open Doors for You to Give Back to Your Community

Jay Mason

Jay Mason (URL: www.vcre.co Email: jay@vcre.co) had a unique blend of work experience before getting his Masters in Elementary Education and a Certification to teach middle school. Now, he works as a real estate agent for Charis Realty Group and enjoys giving back to the community. Although he has always had a strong love of playing sports, he admits that he struggled to find his niche and overcome obstacles. But now he has found fulfillment in the work he does to positively impact people's lives.

How Entrepreneurship Open Doors for You to Give Back to Your Community

One of the many ways Jay has given back to the community is when he once helped a TJ Robotics team. His work helped to expand the program and increase the number of kids who participated. They were able to compete in a few events and actually win Rookie of the Year award in a few of those competitions.

It's work like this that makes Jay proud to be a community liaison. His journey of figuring out what he wanted to do allowed him to learn how he could give back and be a leader, which is something people in corporate jobs don't always have the opportunity to do. He feels that now it's his turn to make a difference and it shows as he's on the Board of Directors for Boys & Girls Club of Frederick County and Habitat for Humanity of Frederick County.

In addition to assisting others, he's also had the opportunity to get to know a diverse group of people throughout the community. He feels that it's his time to help the next wave of students in town. He can show them what it takes to help a community grow and become stronger. It's also a way for him to learn just as much from others as they can learn from him. For Jay, there's nothing better than realizing when it's your moment so you can take the reins and make a difference.

Gaining More Knowledge Through Experience

A book that stands out for Jay is *Outliers* by Malcolm Gladwell. The book talks about how organizations are having to reframe themselves. They are realizing that people have to put in at least 10,000 hours of practice to master a skill. When members of an organization reach this level, they can build a stronger entity.

This revelation has been a defining moment for Jay as he worked to figure out what he wanted to do and where his life was going. Realizing how important it was to set both short-term and long-term goals has been a complete game-changer along his path to success.

ENTREPRENEURSHIP

"Keep on going."

CLARE AHALT

Episode #40 – Clare Ahalt – Photographer

Capturing a Story to Pass Across Generations

Clare Ahalt

Originally from Nottingham, England, Clare Ahalt (http://www.clareahaltphotography.com/ Email: info@clareahaltphotography.com) went to law school in the U.K. She came to the U.S to pursue her Master in International Law at American University Washington College of Law, which is how she ended up in Frederick, Maryland. After graduating, she was hired by the Library of Congress where she became a Foreign Law Specialist.

It wasn't until Clare had her first child that she ventured into the world of photography. With her family living in a different country, she had to find a way for her parents and grandparents to see what her children looked like. She got frustrated when she realized that her brother, who had studied photography, always seemed to take better pictures. She decided to study photography herself and apply it to the photos she was taking for her family. She became a professional photographer in 2013.

Capturing a Story to Pass Across Generations

The biggest challenge for Clare was realizing that there was so much more to photography than just pressing the shutter on a camera. You're capturing a story that will pass from generation to generation, so it's crucial to get it right.

As with any other business, photography involves marketing and accounting, but it also includes knowing how to pose people along with editing pictures. For Clare, this aspect is so important to her because she feels that photography increases in value over time. Grandparents will show their grandkids what they looked like as children.

You're capturing a single moment in time that you can't ever get back. This is especially important when those photos contain loved ones who are no longer with us. It can have an emotional impact on people once they see that photo for the first time.

It's part of Clare's business to work with her clients to capture exactly what they want to see in the photo. Again, you're capturing a specific moment for them so you want to make sure it's how they want to be portrayed.

"Keep on Going."

When Clare was going through her exams in comprehensive school, she paused at one moment to take a break. As one of her teachers walked past her, he said under his breath to her, "Just keep going, Clare."

From that moment forward, any tough moment she's had whether it was an exam in law school or anytime things got tricky, she's recalled that phrase to get her through it. It works well to push her past the hard parts, so she's able to keep going.

"Live daringly, boldly, fearlessly. Taste the relish that can be found in competition – in having put forth the best within you." Henry J. Kaiser

---

RICH AUSTIN

ENTREPRENEURSHIP

Episode #41 – Rich Austin – Trembling Giant Marketing

Five Benefits to Working with a Marketing Company

Rich Austin

After spending most of his life in New Jersey, Rich Austin (URL: https://www.tremblinggiantmarketing.com/) moved to Maryland after graduating college in 2001. He started off studying design at the School of Visual Arts in New York City, but then things took an interesting turn. He transferred out of that program and ended up getting a degree in History at Cornell University! He thought by expanding his knowledge of history that he would have a greater perspective as an artist. Apparently, his strategy worked as he's continued to succeed in the fields of graphic design and marketing.

Another interesting twist in Rich's career came about when he had the opportunity to partner with a friend who had his own marketing agency. When his friend had something come up in his life where he had to take things in another direction, the partnership ended up being an acquisition!

Five Benefits to Working with a Marketing Agency

Rich is always happy to help business owners take a generic logo or business site and transform them into something that represents their actual brand to make a bigger impact. He mentioned that this is just one of many reasons why businesses should work with a professional marketing agency.

Other reasons he states include:

1. Consistency – An agency can provide a full solution instead of just a single portion of one. By having a complete go-to creative team, you can have the same voice, look, and feel across all of your marketing collateral.

The more you work with them, the more you can work with a team who knows what you're looking for, which will save you time and effort in the long run.
2. Flexibility – You can have more options by working with an agency. Because of the relationships they have with media outlets, you can have access to platforms you might not have been aware of without having to pay a middleman fee to use them.
3. Expert Advice & Experience – Most businesses don't have experience in-house with marketing and advertising. With an agency, you can let them handle those details while you can focus on what you do best. Plus, with their expertise, they can assist you with figuring out a solution that works best for you.
4. Quality Across the Board – With most small businesses, budgets are tight, especially for a fully developed marketing strategy. Instead of paying individual rates for a social media guru, content writer, or copywriter, you can gain access to all three with an agency at a much more affordable price.
5. Role in the Community – When you use a local agency like Rich's, you increase the chances of helping out your local community. Most agencies will look to support those individuals and businesses who are also local, which benefits the community where you live and work.

Since converting his friend's company into Trembling Giant Marketing in December 2014, Rich has been growing ever since. He prides himself on the team he's built over the years, especially because they do all stem from the local community. Not only does his business support other businesses in the area, but he's also providing an income for the lives of the people who work in the community as well.

ENTREPRENEURSHIP

"If you're not ridiculously excited about what you're doing, it's time to change it."

LAURA WALLACE

BEYOND THE MIC

Episode #42 – Laura Wallace – Worx

Why Your Business Needs to Create a Brand Experience

Laura Wallace

Laura Wallace (URL: http://worxgraphicdesign.com/) was born and raised in Pennsylvania but grew up in Maryland. She lived in MD for a while but graduated from and lives in PA currently. Her business is in MD now and Laura, the owner of Worx, a graphic design firm for the last ten years. She initially started out doing graphic design at the Yellow Pages, which taught her how to work with clients as well as the concept of deadlines. It wasn't until her and her husband decided to start a family that she realized she wanted to make a change. She started doing freelance on the side, and when she was six-months pregnant, she quit her job to start her business!

Laura also has a similar platform to my own podcast called the Green Couch Project (URL: http://www.thegreencouchproject.com/). I encourage you to check it out as it's a platform where entrepreneurs can "spill their gutsy" and talk about their struggles and how they've overcome them. It's a great source of inspiration for those days when things may not be going the way you expect them to.

Why Your Business Needs to Create a Brand Experience

Laura is fully aware that talking about "brand" can often be confusing for business owners. Most people know what they want for their business but aren't sure of how to visualize it. As a graphic designer, it's her job to encourage business owners to think about what their brand is. What many don't realize is that brand goes well beyond a logo, colors you use, and what your ads look like.

In reality, your brand should be emotion-based. It's how people will feel when they work or interact with you. It's how they speak about your business when you're not around. It's also who you are to them, and how you make a difference to them.

Regardless of your business size, you can create a brand experience simply by staying true to who you are. Spreading this message consistently across all platforms with a familiar look and feel will create that experience. All too often, Laura will see a business site that is very fun and quirky, but when she talks to the people in the business, they are conservative and low-key. This can create a brand disconnect with your audience, which is what firms like Worx can help with.

And if you're worried about attracting the right people to work with, Laura says not to be. If you create a brand experience by being yourself, you will naturally attract those people who are meant to work with you. It's those people who are like-minded who will become your best and most loyal clients.

Being Resilient and Open to Change

Laura points to the book, *Successful Women Think Differently* by Valerie Burton, as a resource that resonates with her. In the book, it talks about being resilient and being able to bounce back. It also stresses being authentic and staying true to your calling.

A quote that she's always referring to is one of her own. "If you're not ridiculously excited about what you're doing, it's time to change it." It's actually something that can be applied any day and to any situation. Laura states that it can be a good way for people to consider when it might be time to make a change and live according to what's best for you.

"When you plug into the energy of the crowd, you kind of become almost one."

ALEX SINCEVICH

ENTREPRENEURSHIP

Episode #48 – Alex Sincevich – The Dapper DJ's

Using Classic Music to Build a Modern Business

Alex Sincevich

Alex Sincevich (http://thedapperdjs.com/) is proud to call Frederick, Maryland his hometown. He started deejaying with a friend in high school where they did basement parties for friends. But it was one Christmas that changed everything. He didn't have anything to give his mother as a present, so he decided to refurbish her Victrola as a gift. It led him to start playing old records from his family's collection, and he wanted to include classic music as part of his DJ business and take it on the road. At first, he started playing on the streets, and then he was able to build his business up from there. Now he works with his brother Jack, and they perform at special events and weddings.

Using Classic Music to Build a Modern Business

What Alex wants people to know is that deejaying is so much more than playing music. It's about becoming part of the energy of the people in the room. You're the one getting the people to dance and enjoy themselves.

Most of the process involves finding the right mix. By being able to read the crowd, you can play the right music at the right time to create and enhance the party atmosphere. It also helps if the DJ can plug into the energy of the crowd and become one with the group. Any room can ebb and flow, and it's up to a good DJ to ride that wave.

What makes Alex's business unique from other DJ businesses is that it is based on use of a Victrola, and most people aren't familiar with this type of music player. Plus, he's found a way to incorporate music from as early as the 1910's.

His business is also helping younger generations get introduced to not only the type of music from this era but also how that music was played. Nowhere was this more true when he performed for his son's class at school. Of course, he led them in singing the Hokey Pokey and the Bunny Hop, but that wasn't what was fascinating to them. The fact that the Victrola doesn't require electricity was just one part of their amazement. The other part was the vinyl records he was playing. When he explained to them that it was like a CD, but only bigger, most of them didn't even know what that was!

It brings to mind that in our digital age, some of our treasured mementos from just a decade or so are disappearing. I love the fact that Alex's business is helping to keep those memories alive from not just our generation but that of our parent's and grandparent's as well.

Fine Tuning Your Brand

A godsend for Alex's business was when he read *Brandstarter*™ by Laura Wallace (see Episode 42). He credits the workbook for helping him to put all his thoughts down on paper. It helped him to fine tune his brand, and it made everything click to help him build a successful business.

ENTREPRENEURSHIP

"Smile and enjoy every day as Friday."

JASON LEE

Episode #52 – Jason Lee – Lee Building Maintenance

The True Benefits of a Cleaning Company

Jason Lee

Jason Lee (http://leebuildingclean.com/) has seen a lot of change over the years in Frederick, Maryland as he's lived here his whole life. He's one of those people that was born an entrepreneur and has actually been one for at least the last fifteen years. In high school, he always dreamed of doing something big, and he found a way to make that dream come true.

It all started when he was working at Burger King and watched the vendor who would come in to clean the windows. He started asking them questions about their business and quickly realized how much of an opportunity it could be for him. The next day he researched where and how to buy window cleaning tools. A few days later, he was knocking on doors to get his first clients.

He also had the fortune to meet a gentleman who encouraged him to join the Building Service Contractors Association International (BSCAI). Lee was skeptical at first until he realized that the man he was talking to was the president of the organization! Once he joined them in 2004, his whole world changed. BSCAI made him realize that he could go beyond the scope of just cleaning windows. With the help of many companies all over the world, he was able to get the mentorship that helped him build what is now Lee Building Maintenance.

The True Benefits of a Cleaning Company

It's no secret that people can be messy. For someone like Lee, that's great news as it means that there are lots of opportunities to clean!

One thing that Lee prides himself on is that he adds a personal touch to the work he does for his clients. It's something he is determined to maintain no matter how big his company grows.

Lee also strives to make sure that the company is community-oriented. They focus on doing good for the people in their community, and it shows in the partnerships they've built with non-profits in the area.

Yet, there's another benefit to the company that one might not have considered. As a low-skill wage business, it can be difficult for their employees to feel good about cleaning something like a toilet. But they don't look at it that way.

Lee encourages his staff by reminding them that they are providing a clean, healthy environment for their clients. The services they provide allow their clients to enjoy a clean space to work and do business in. He wants to ensure that the people who work for him are more than just someone who cleans. He feels that by motivating them, he can encourage them to take pride in their work and keep them moving forward.

Treating Every Day Like Friday

We often hear people say how excited they are in one form or another when it's Friday. But it's something that Lee honestly doesn't understand. To him, we should treat every day like Friday, and then we'll have a reason to smile that much more!

Lee mentions that the book *Make the Noise Go Away* by Larry Linne has been important to him as a business owner. Being your own boss can be a challenge and the book explains how having a "second-in-command" can help to eliminate the noise in your head to protect your ideas and create a stronger organization.

"The true way to make a difference is to leave the world a better place than what it was before you arrived."

MARK STEVANUS

ENTREPRENEURSHIP

Episode #53 – Mark Stevanus – Social Boss

Leveling the Playing Field with Social Media

Mark Stevanus

Even though Mark Stevanus (https://www.socialboss4u.com/) started out in a 9 – 5 job, he didn't let that stop him from taking advantage of opportunities. He worked at the Department of Energy for almost thirteen years and learned a lot during that time. Although, he also knew that he didn't want to be there forever.

He learned a lot about technology there, and it's also where he learned how to code for websites. He got burnt out and was always interested in entrepreneurship. He took a leap of faith like most other entrepreneurs and started a web design business. Initially, he helped non-profit businesses, and it's how he developed his love for social media. He then sold his company to start Social Boss, so he could focus on helping his clients with social media.

Leveling the Playing Field with Social Media

The one thing that makes Mark love social media so much is that it levels the playing field. The smaller companies can gain just as much leverage online as the bigger companies by having an online presence.

Social media gives businesses a platform where they have the opportunity to tell their unique, incredible story and share it with the world. It's the perfect way for him to help his clients succeed.

As Mark points out, everyone has the same amount of time in a day, so there's no excuse for not getting your business out there. They all have access to social media, and with it, he can help them figure out a plan that suits their business. He can work with them to develop a strategy that shows what to post, when to post it, and how to use social media to attract the right audience for their business.

In addition to social media, he uses tactics like video marketing so that his clients have access to a range of tools to choose from to take their business to the next level. He also provides free tips on his blog and for his social media followers to help his clients. These posts often include interviews with other businesses, so that others can learn what steps they took to find their own success online.

Leaving the World a Better Place

Mark says that one of his own quotes is very important to him. "The true way to make a difference is to leave the world a better place than what it was before you arrived." For him, this philosophy makes you focus on the good and on doing the right thing. We're all put on this earth to help others and to enjoy life. It's our opportunity to get out there and do it.

"Opportunity is missed by people because it's dressed in overalls and looks like work."

KELSEY FREEMAN

Episode #55 – Kelsey Freeman – Forefront Digital Media

Working with a Social Media Marketing Consultant

Kelsey Freeman

Even though Kelsey Freeman (http://forefrontdigitalmedia.com/) was almost destined to be a teacher, her path seems to have naturally turned towards social media and helping others. At her kindergarten graduation, she said she wanted to be a teacher and never wavered on it. However, once she graduated from college and started teaching, Kelsey got frustrated with the education system when she realized that her love of English didn't always pass on to her students.

She decided to go back to graduate school and get her Masters in communication. This action stemmed from a goal for her students. She wanted them to be able to speak, read, or write well as those would be life skills that would get them somewhere along their career path no matter what. As part of her grad school work, she was required to do internships that would instigate major changes in her life. Her political communication internship made an impact on her, and she really appreciated her teacher.

Kelsey's internship in politics brought her to Annapolis where she was hired by the County Executives' Office and worked with State Delegates as a community and public relations director. What most people may not realize is that delegates often have their own careers and they have to split that responsibility with their government work. When them delegates saw what Kelsey was able to do to keep them connected with their constituents through social media, they started asking her to apply the same strategies to their businesses. And that's how she started her social media consulting business, Forefront Digital Media.

ENTREPRENEURSHIP

Working with a Social Media Marketing Consultant

For Kelsey, the biggest challenge with her business is that some people are intimidated by social media, or they've been successful in business for a while and feel like they don't need it. She has to explain to them that social media isn't as difficult as it might seem and it's not something that will replace existing marketing tactics. It works to enhance what businesses already have in place and creates an online presence where they can interact with their audience.

In fact, Kelsey feels that social media is much more about public relations than marketing. You're developing relationships and branding yourself. By having a conversation with your audience, you're building an online presence, not just promoting your business. It's also your customer's outlet for being able to communicate with you, which is why it's so important to keep an eye on reviews and get in front of any potential issues that could turn into a nightmare.

Kelsey also doesn't believe in standardized packages for her business as everyone's needs are different. She creates customized packages for her clients that reflect their goals and the audience they're trying to reach.

Given her teaching background, it shouldn't come as a surprise that Kelsey also offers comprehensive training sessions for her clients. She considers it a full educational experience where she gives you goals to reach and challenges to help you figure out what you're doing and how to make it a success.

Opportunity is Everywhere

Kelsey has a fun quote that her grandfather used to tell her about opportunity. "Opportunity is missed by people because it's dressed in overalls and looks like work." The quote basically serves as a reminder that opportunity is everywhere. Sometimes you may have to work for it, but it will come to light as something worthwhile. As

Kelsey says, don't just pass something by because it involves work, you never know what the end result could be.

"I've learned that people will forget what you said, people will forget what you did, but people will never forget how you made them feel." Maya Angelou

WHITNEY HAHN

BEYOND THE MIC

Episode #59 – Whitney Hahn – Digital Bard Video

Promoting Businesses Through the Power of Storytelling

Whitney Hahn

Whitney Hahn (URL: https://www.digitalbard.com/ Email: whitney@digitalbard.com) had the opportunity to experience entrepreneurship from a young age. Her parents owned the Catoctin Wildlife Preserve and Zoo. In fact, the house she grew up in was in the middle of the zoo, so on her way to the bus stop, she passed the alligators and squirrel monkeys to get there. It also made for fun sleepovers, as the animals made their own unique sounds throughout the day and night.

When she was 13, Whitney also worked at the zoo showing people tarantulas up close or letting them pet the baby alligators. She attributes this experience as what led her on the path she's on today. She loved seeing people's initial reaction to something they hadn't seen before, and that still holds true now with her business, Digital Bard Video.

Promoting Businesses Through the Power of Storytelling

As Whitney points out, storytelling has been around since humankind drew pictures on the walls of caves and sat around the fire at night. She already knew the power of story through her work at the zoo as well as a career in radio and as a host of the TV show the Wild Life on GS Communications. When she saw that environment changing, she and the producer of the show decided to start Digital Bard Video, so they could communicate stories in the way that was important to them.

In addition to helping businesses and organizations tell their story online, they also help with creating a strategy behind the marketing campaign. With the popularity of online platforms like YouTube, it's essential for businesses to have a storytelling aspect to their promotional efforts.

Whitney's team believes highly experiential brands deserve video. Thier work with leisure and entertainment brands is focused on capturing the visual richness of the visitor environment along with the joyful laughter, screams of delight, sighs of relaxation or satisfied "yummy" sounds of a guest enjoying the experience.

Whitney feels that it's an honor when one of her clients trusts her with their story. It's a very rewarding experience for her as she loves to see their reaction when they see their story reflected back to them for the very first time.

Being Cool with Who You Are

Even though Whitney says that she reads a ton of books, especially business-related texts, I made her choose one that stands out to her as a great resource. She mentioned that the book, *You Are a Badass* by Jen Sincero, is one that she refers to the most. It shows you the way to be cool with who you are. The universe is constantly working on your behalf, and it's your job to let it. It's a book that she read when she wasn't sure entrepreneurship was right for her, and it's also one that she gifts to others as well.

"Do unto others as you would have done to you."

MONICA STUCKEY

ENTREPRENEURSHIP

Episode #61 – Monica Stuckey – ML Stuckey Consulting

How a Twist of Fate Led to a Thriving Business

Monica Stuckey

Monica Stuckey (https://www.mlstuckeyconsulting.com/) grew up in Damascus, Maryland and went to college at Virginia Tech. Her passion is with helping animals, which shows in her work with Uniting to Save Animals, a local non-profit that provides low-cost spay and neuter services in the Frederick, Maryland area.

Monica spent 15 years working for MRIS (Metropolitan Regional Information Systems), also known as the arm of the MLS or where all the real estate listings come from. The company was going through a merger, and she ended up being laid off. They did offer her the opportunity to interview for a promotion, but having just been in a car accident and suffering from a severe concussion, she decided that it wasn't the best option for her. While she was home recuperating, someone approached her with doing a website for them for pay, and she decided to start her own business.

How a Twist of Fate Led to a Thriving Business

As Monica says, "I wouldn't have started my own company if I had been in my right mind." However, she views it as a good thing because she might never have taken the leap. And she can't be happier that she did!

In fact, Monica wishes she had taken the opportunity to start sooner because she enjoys helping people with their businesses. One time, she worked with a business who had been having terrible issues with their website. They went from one company to the next, and things went from bad to worse. Due to some black hat tactics, their site was showing on the 50th page on Google even though the companies they were working with promised page one search results.

Monica was able to transform their site and remove the black hat techniques. Now, they are on page one or two on Google and still improving. They had lost quite a bit of their business due to the mishap, and Monica loves the fact that she was able to help them.

For her, it's more than just about revamping or creating a website. Her work involves learning her customer's pain points and identifying how she can solve them. She looks at what is working as well as what isn't to get a complete overview of what's going on with their site. She then shows them how she can get them what they need through her step-by-step process.

The Book Everyone Should Read

Monica states that everyone should read the book, *The Giving Tree* by Shel Silverstein. Even though it's a children's book, she feels that it's a concept we should all understand and it's how she lives her life.

She also refers to the quote "Do unto others as you would have done to you," as a phrase that's important to her. It covers all aspects of life from family, friends, co-workers, and clients and it's embodied in how she treats people.

ENTREPRENEURSHIP

"The best time to plant a tree is 20 years ago. The second-best time is right now." Old Chinese proverb

SCOTT ALEXANDER

BEYOND THE MIC

Episode #64 – Scott Alexander – Scott Alexander Consulting

Leadership is a State of Being

Scott Alexander

Scott Alexander (http://www.scottmalexander.com/) is a third-generation Fredericktonian. He has spent over 25 years in various leadership positions and has a unique ability to see people where they are, where they're headed, and how to help them take the next step on that path.

It was when Scott left his last CEO position that he had the opportunity to do some soul searching and explore his options. Being in his 40's combined with the unexpected death of his father changed his perspective. People approached him about how his dad, a local businessman, had influenced their lives and it led him to ask himself, "What do I have to offer others?"

Instead of taking another job, he decided to write a book titled, Lead Like a Black Belt™, which stemmed from his leadership skills and extensive experience in martial arts. Since that book was published in 2014, Scott has been helping people do business in a different way.

Leadership is a State of Being

According to Scott, a really important lesson for people to learn is that leadership isn't a set of skills; it's a state of being. You can't just read a bunch of books and automatically become a leader. Leadership is a complex way of looking at the world and interacting with people.

It's Scott's work that helps people become intentional about how they influence others. Any leader will have influence, but is what they're doing matching their intentions? Are they moving people in the right direction that they want them to go? And are they doing that on purpose or is it simply a by-product of their situation?

In business, we all have a strategy. Whether it's building houses, doing taxes, or selling insurance, there's a strategy behind it. To do that, we also build a structure through how we work and who we work with. Those people that we hire to work with will create a culture within the business. As a leader, it's important to ensure that the structure is aligned with the strategy and that the culture is aligned with both. Once that's in place, the business is more profitable, and its employees are happy to work there.

Overall, leadership is the difference between making money and being successful. We can have a company where everyone is going in the same direction, people are happy to be there, and there's a balance between their work, and what they get out of it. A successful company will have all of those elements combined.

Creating Your Next Opportunity

Scott likes the quote, "The best time to build a tree is 20 years ago. The second-best time is right now."

It tells you that foresight is important. Life takes time, and that for a "tree" to grow and develop, it takes 20 years. But, it's not about lamenting about missed opportunities, just create the next one. It also serves as a "get moving" message and begs the question: What's stopping you from planting a tree right now?

"Every morning in Africa, a gazelle wakes up and knows that it must run faster than the fastest lion or it will be killed and eaten. Also, every morning in Africa, a lion wakes up and knows it must outrun the slowest gazelle or it will starve to death. It doesn't matter if you are the lion or the gazelle when the sun comes up, you better start running."
From a *Setback is a Setup for a Comeback* by Willie Jolley

ANTOINE THOMAS

ENTREPRENEURSHIP

Episode #66 – Antoine Thomas – ATQ Cleaning

How a Plan "B" Turned into a Growing, Successful Business

Antione Thomas

Antoine Thomas (https://www.facebook.com/ATQCleaning/) grew up together in Frederick, Maryland. His career with a biotech company took a turn when the business was in the process of being bought out. Even though he was informed that no one in his department would be laid off, two people lost their jobs anyway.

It was a defining moment for Antoine, and he realized that he needed to come up with a plan "B" to ensure that he could make a living. He had seen friends like Jason Lee (Chapter #52) start their cleaning companies and it inspired him to start his own. He opened his cleaning business in 2009 and just recently branched out to offer more services such as residential carpet cleaning for houses, apartments, and townhomes.

How a Plan "B" Turned into a Growing, Successful Business

Antoine knew his cleaning company was taking off as he started getting more calls from businesses within the community. At that point, he was able to work full-time on it, so he could better serve his clients.

Antoine knows the business and prides himself on having a professional cleaning company with workers who are skilled with cleaning, dusting, and sanitizing. He also likes educating his clients on what to do and what not to do to have a cleaner environment.

But Antoine's business goes beyond just cleaning. He also says that some business owners may delegate unwanted cleaning duties to their staff, which can cause morale to drop. Also, because they may not want to handle that responsibility, they may not do as good of a job. Instead, his team can come into a business and take care of all of their cleaning needs so that the owner and staff can do the work they do best.

Hiring a professional cleaning company can also prevent dust build-up, which can prevent respiratory issues. When surfaces like blinds are kept clean and free of dust, it can be beneficial to people who have allergies and help prevent people from getting sick. Not only is this good for the staff and their family, but it's also good for the company's productivity.

"...You Better Start Running."

Antoine states that the book, *A Setback is a Setup for a Comeback* by Willie Jolley as a source of inspiration for him. The above quote reminds him that you have to be ready to get going every morning. It's something he lives by and feels that every day is an opportunity. It's also what keeps him asking "What can I do better with my business to help someone else with theirs?"

ENTREPRENEURSHIP

"No one ever cries when you give them a Compliment."

JORDAN LEWIS

Episode #67 – Jordan Lewis – JKW Beauty

Instilling Confidence with Color

Jordan Lewis

Having a mom who was a small business owner gave Jordan Lewis (http://jkwbeauty.com/) insight into what entrepreneurship would be like. It was when she went off to college that she realized that she didn't know what she wanted to do with her life. She decided to take a break, and her father suggested that she take a semester off to find something she liked and to learn about it.

She wanted to do something creative, and since there weren't any interior design classes at that time, she took a makeup artistry class. No one was more surprised than she was regarding her choice as she never really was into the beauty realm. After the class, she applied for a job at MAC Cosmetics and was hired. Three years later she had moved into a management role but was ready for a change.

She took what she learned from the service side of the cosmetics business and started her own mobile glam squad. There was nothing like it at the time, but after hundreds of weddings and other special events, she now considers herself an expert.

Instilling Confidence with Color

If you ask Jordan, she will tell you that makeup is much more than just an accessory. For her, it's a way of instilling confidence through the use of color. She can use the combination of color, contour, and art in a way to enhance a person's features. In a way, it's like fashion. When people put it on, they feel good about themselves.

Given the fact that Jordan works so close to her clients, she gets to know people on an intimate level. It helps them to open up and share their tastes, so she can decide on the best makeup and hairstyle to match with what they want. It not only builds relationships, but it also helps Jordan to showcase that person's personality and individuality.

Jordan also likes to emphasize that her work doesn't just involve applying a product on someone or changing their appearance. Instead, she likes to think of it as enhancing what's already present within the person.

"No One Every Cries When You Give Them a Compliment"

That quote comes from Jordan herself. It stood out during our conversation, and I encouraged her to claim it as a reflection of what she does. It shows exactly how the work she does can instill confidence. She also loves the fact that she is helping others to feel good about themselves. Jordan also likes the following quote by Camille Pissarro, "Blessed are those who see beautiful things in humble places where other people see nothing."

"It is not enough to have this globe or a certain time. I will have thousands of globes and all time." From the poem 'A Song of Joys' by Walt Whitman

---

JESSICA MCHUGH

ENTREPRENEURSHIP

Episode #69 – Jessica McHugh – Writer & Author

The Power of Using Pen & Paper

Jessica McHugh

Growing up in Hampstead, Maryland, Jessica McHugh (http://www.jessicamchughbooks.com/) loved being surrounded by woods where she would often go to read. Later on, her active imagination would lead her to pursue theatre and choir opportunities. After jumping from one college to the next, Jessica stopped going, but she never lost her love her reading and writing.

At 19, she was working in a kiosk in the mall where she sold perfume 11 hours a day making minimum wage. Thankfully, there was a Waldenbooks nearby where she would go and buy a book to help her pass the time. She was heavily into short story and anthology collections, especially in the horror and fantasy genres, and read a variety of authors including Roald Dahl, H.P. Lovecraft, and J.R.R. Tolkien.

The Power of Using Pen & Paper

Reading so many short stories inspired Jessica to write her own. Even though she admits that at first, they weren't very good, they made for a good, jumping off point to start writing. In addition to her short stories, she also tried her hand at creating a new world and inventing a new language for a fantasy novel.

Even from the early days at the perfume kiosk when she first started writing, Jessica never thought of her writing as a career or publishing her work. She fell in love with the writing and never wanted to stop. In fact, she says that she'll do any job as long as she can write.

The interesting thing I discovered with Jessica that in spite of all the technological advances, she writes the first draft of her books by hand. And she has a stack of notebooks to prove it! For her, writing pen to paper offers a visceral sense of the story compared to typing or just telling it out loud. She likens it to painting where you're making the page come alive with words. Even if you don't know what you're trying to say, the story will take its own shape.

As Jessica points out, language is a vast, complicated thing. The way you can take words and put them all together to create rhythm, dance, and music on the page. That combined with the way you format it is all a form of art.

One of the things that surprised Jessica the most with her writing career is how she has embraced the horror genre. She's not one to like scary movies and admits that she gets scared easily, but still loves writing it. She makes the observation that everyone has experienced some form of horror in their lives, and it doesn't have to be about blood and gore. Whether it's being scared of heights, spiders, being stabbed, or just going on a first date, we can all identify with it.

Living With a Crazy Imagination

Jessica takes inspiration from a snippet of the poem "A Song of Joys" by Walt Whitman. "It is not enough to have this globe or a certain time. I will have thousands of globes and all time." For Jessica, she could never be okay with being a "normal chick." It never interested her to be the type to get up, go to work, come home, and repeat the process day after day. She's always lived with a crazy imagination and perpetually wanted to be someone else. She is able to live in all "globes and times" through writing fiction and by creating so many characters, worlds, personalities, and experiences.

She also varies her writing from serious stuff to silly stuff and everything in-between. It also helps that she's able to channel her own frustrations and joys into her characters.

ENTREPRENEURSHIP

"A family that prays together, stays together."
Patrick Peyton

HAROLD BUSSEY JR.

Episode #70 – Harold Bussey, Jr. – ZCZ Cleaning Company

Overcoming Setbacks to Create a Legacy

Harold Bussey, Jr.

Growing up in Brooklyn, New York, Harold Bussey, Jr. (http://zczfamilycleaningservices.com/) learned early on how to overcome setbacks. He feels humbled and blessed that he's been able to take advantage of opportunities that led him out of his old neighborhood to bring him to where he is now. He's also grateful to those people that kept him in line with where he needed to go with his life.

Harold started working with the New York City Housing Authority right out of high school, which was where he first learned about the cleaning atmosphere. Although he went on to work with several different companies, all of them involved some aspect of cleaning. At one point, something came over him, and he realized the importance of starting his own company. His thought process was that he wouldn't know what could happen unless he tried it. He also knew the best place to start was with something he knew, and ZCZ Family Cleaning Company was born.

Overcoming Setbacks to Create a Legacy

As most business owners know, starting a business is not to be taken lightly. Many struggles and challenges present themselves along the way that we often don't have control over. For Harold, it was a few different setbacks in addition to a personal tragedy within his family that caused him to second-guess what he was doing.

Even though that time was filled with depression and darkness, he was able to prevail and turned the negatives into positives. It also made him realize that he needed to live each day to the fullest and accomplish things that others may never have the chance to do.

Harold's main objective with his business is to leave something for his three children. He wants them to have something to build on for when they get older and is already involving them in the business.

He has a unique approach to his business in that he works with his clients on a more personal level than you would expect from a cleaning company. He focuses on getting to know people first, discovers their strengths, and build trust. Once that happens, he then discusses how he can help them. Whether it's just cleaning services in general or how he can help them save time, he wants to help his clients approach cleaning in a more efficient manner.

Inspiration from Family

A quote that stays with Harold and one that he has instilled in his family is, "A family that prays together stays together." It's a concept that comes directly from his grandmother, and he credits it for what has molded him into the man he is today. His belief is that by praying together, his family can work together and stay together no matter what.

BEYOND THE MIC

"It's not about me."

ADAM BRADLEY

ENTREPRENEURSHIP

Episode #73 – Adam Bradley – Lead 'Em Up/Hardwood Hustle

Helping People Develop a Leadership Mindset

Adam Bradley

Adam Bradley (http://leademup.com/) claims himself as a "Maryland guy through and through." He grew up in Montgomery County, Maryland and still has close relationships with his buddies from high school. He loves spending time with them and with his family in addition to working on not one, but TWO businesses!

Helping People Develop a Leadership Mindset

When Adam first ventured into entrepreneurship, he started what would eventually become Hardwood Hustle from a friend's basement. The online sports network they created started out covering just the Redskins. Due to its success, he ended up working out deals with the Wizards and Capitals. The platform gave him the opportunity to interview and meet with people from RG3 to local high school coaches.

One of those coaches recommended that they do a podcast, named Hardwood Hustle. The combination of sponsors and the coach's big social media presence allowed them to build a successful business centered around coaching. With their success, they had the ability to be influential and impact people in a positive light.

But his success didn't end there. Adam's popularity grew, and he was asked to start speaking at high schools, companies, and various events. When he spoke at his former high school, one of the coaches approached him to talk to the team once a week and help with motivating them. He quickly realized that once a week wouldn't be enough, so he started spending more time with the team. This experience forced him to document his processes and come up with content on a regular basis. Through that content, he was able to support them through their struggles and inspire them with what was to become his 12-week program, the beginning of Lead 'Em Up.

It's through his program that he can help groups work towards a greater good. He shows leaders of all types that goals and objectives won't get accomplished unless everyone comes together as a team. That means that a leader and the team have to be synced in a leadership mindset, and it's his job to figure out how to help them get there.

The level of work he goes through requires everyone involved to be intentional. He provides them with the curriculum to take that intention and take part in a step-by-step, powerful, fun, dynamic leadership program. The program is one that will challenge, push, and grow the team so that by the end of the 12 weeks, they will see incredible growth.

Growing Relationships with Others

As the head of a leadership development company, Adam knows how important it is to build relationships. He cites the book, *Never Eat Alone* by Keith Ferrazzi as one that helps him with relationships. It talks about how you can build on the power of relationships and connect with others in both your personal and professional life.

Adam also likes the saying, "It's not about me." With his business, it isn't about him. It's about his impact on other people. He loves that he can share what he's been through with other people and how he can help make them shine.

"Don't ask what the world needs. Ask what makes you come alive and go do it. Because what the world needs is people who have come alive."
Robert Thurman

JANICE RILEY

BEYOND THE MIC

Episode #74 – Janice Riley – The Technical Innovation Center at Howard Community College

Helping Entrepreneurs Make Them Dream Come to Life

Janice Riley

Growing up on a fruit farm and picking apples, potatoes, and strawberries taught Janice Riley (http://www.hagerstowncc.edu/department/technical-innovation-center) the importance of doing things right the first time. Between that, weeding gardens, and tree trimming, she also learned a good work ethic.

After graduating with a Bachelors in Marketing, Janice started her own consulting business, which centered on strategic marketing for startups and small businesses. Her experience led her to work on a project with a software startup. The startup was doing a marketing outreach for the National Space Grant, which is NASA's outreach program for colleges. She worked on the program for four years. When they started, it was just four kids in a basement. By the time she left, it was a mix of 50 employees and contractors.

She decided to go back into the startup world and received a call from the dean of continuing education at Hagerstown Community College. They had seen her resume and wanted to interview her for a job at the Technical Innovation Center's Business incubator, and the rest is history.

Janice now works with entrepreneurs to help them take their ideas and bring them to life. She works with them side by side and strategizes a plan to build their business. She takes the time to go over their options and how to make it all happen. In addition to planning, she can also connect entrepreneurs with valuable resources.

Janice acts as a liaison service portal so that businesses can connect with various local economic offices, financial resources, and service providers. During her conversation with the entrepreneur, she will determine what they need help with. If she can't help them, she will connect them with a resource who can. Most of the time, those resources are at no cost to the entrepreneur.

The facility provides office space, manufacturer floor space, and research labs as part of their services. They also hold seminars and workshops that are open to the public.

Passion for Your Work

Janice turns to the quote by Robert Thurman, "Don't ask what the world needs. Ask what makes you come alive, and go do it. Because what the world needs is people who have come alive," as a source of inspiration. Every day she sees people who have a passion that is so important to them that they want to turn it into a reality. You have to have a passion for what you're doing, and if you don't, why are you doing it?

"It is what it is."

TREY WILKES

ENTREPRENEURSHIP

Episode #75 – Trey Wilkes – The Lax Factory

Helping Kids Succeed in Sports and Life

Trey Wilkes

Trey Wilkes is Frederick County born and raised and currently living in Baltimore, Maryland. He's partnered with Dr. Josh Funk (see Chapter #71) at the Lax Factory to help kids succeed in the community.

He initially started working with Dr. Josh as part of a program that helped boys at the sixth, seventh, and eighth-grade levels. Both of them had a desire to teach kids the game of lacrosse. Each year another team was added, and his role was with coaching the older kids. When Dr. Josh saw how Trey was handling the business, he let him run with it so that he could focus on his physical therapy clinic, Rehab 2 Perform.

Helping Kids Succeed in Sports and Life

Originally, Trey had gone into medical sales and thought he wanted to just sell and make money. He quickly realized that wasn't the person he wanted to be. He never even saw himself as a businessperson but enjoyed working with the kids and being a part of their progress.

Trey attributes specific aspects of the Lax Factory that works to make a difference in the kid's lives. First, they're big on leadership. And that's where he also partners up with Adam Bradley (see Chapter #73). Adam provides them with a curriculum that teaches the kids to become leaders. With all the distractions kids have in our current society, it's important to give the opportunity to learn leadership skills. It's not always the person in the middle of a huddle cheering everyone on. Sometimes the leader is someone on the sidelines helping to pick someone up when they're down. Or, the person who sees a peer struggling and goes out of their way to help them out.

Trey and his team also focus heavily on academics. They require that the kids in their program maintain a 3.0 or higher GPA or they'll have to leave the program. If anyone slips, they refund any money, and ban them from attending so they can turn their focus towards academics. He will then work with school counselors and teachers to help them get on the right path. And the same philosophy goes for the recruiting process. Trey won't recommend recruiting any of the athletes if their GPA falls below the 3.0 mark.

Player development is also a key part of their program. They work with second grade to eighth-grade kids, and they practice more than any other program available in the state. They practice four days out of the week, with one of those days focused on films. On Saturdays and Sundays, they are playing in the number one league in the country. All of their staff have either played or coached at the college level, which works towards constant development for the kids to be the best players they can be. They also encourage playing other sports besides lacrosse as this experience directly correlates to enhanced success on the field.

The Lax Factory also provides recruiting and networking services. Trey works with college coaches every day and trains the kids to succeed at the college level. Once the kids return home from college or finish a summer internship, he also works with them to help them find work in the community.

Keep Moving Forward & Looking Ahead

Trey references two quotes that are important to him, and he refers to them as the family quote and the work quote. For the family quote, he credits his sister with the popular saying, "It is what it is." In her early teens, she had suffered a third torn ACL injury. His entire family was upset, but she stayed strong and realized that no one could change what had happened. All she could do was keep moving forward.

ENTREPRENEURSHIP

The work quote that Trey likes is, "The next play." We can't worry about what's already happened. We have to focus on what's coming next. It's important to understand that not everything in life is going to be a win. We will lose sometimes, but it's those moments where we need to figure out what we're going to do next.

BEYOND THE MIC

CLOSING STATEMENT

A Good Book Has No Ending. – RD Cumming

Closing

BEYOND THE MIC
Stories from the Everyday Entrepreneur

Thank you for investing your time into *Beyond the Mic*. I hope that you enjoyed reading each person's story.

For every guest on *Frederick Advice Givers*, their heart and soul goes into their businesses EVERY DAY. They bring such a passion into what they do for you that I only find it fitting to help them share their Story with you in as many platforms as possible.

If just one of these Stories resonated with you and maybe gave you something to think about, then I've accomplished the job of introducing you to a new person, strategy, or business that you didn't know existed before *Beyond the Mic*.

If you want to learn more about anyone featured in this book, it's simple, go to www.FrederickAdviceGivers.com and then type in a forward slash and the guests first and last name. It will take you directly to their interview.

If you, yourself are an Entrepreneur, Business Owner, or thought-leader and you would like to share your story with the world, then head over to www.FrederickPodcastBooking.com to apply to be interviewed for the podcast.

Thanks so much for reading *Beyond the Mic*!

Eric Verdi

CLOSING

www.ingramcontent.com/pod-product-compliance
Lightning Source LLC
Chambersburg PA
CBHW052144220526
45471CB00004B/1519